'What [Downing] saw an...
remarkable now, but was...
What is exceptional is how he wrote about it.'

Bill Gammage
The Age

'a superbly-written first-hand account of the horrors of World War I in the trenches.'

Jim Tennison
The Herald Sun

'Downing's book is compelling.'

Tony Stephens
The Sydney Morning Herald

'Spare, beautiful in its clarity, and heart-breakingly vivid.'

The Courier-Mail

'If you read nothing else about Australians in war, read *To the Last Ridge*.'

Peter Henning
The Examiner

To Dear Dad

Merry Christmas 98

Lots of love

Tim + Mikey

XXX

To the Last Ridge

W.H. Downing

DUFFY & SNELLGROVE
SYDNEY

Published by Duffy & Snellgrove 1998
PO Box 177 Potts Point NSW 2011 Australia
dands@magna.com.au

Reprinted in 1998

First published in 1920 by H.H. Champion. Australasian
Author's Agency, Melbourne

Distributed by Tower Books (02) 9975 5566

Roll of Honour and Nominal Roll gratefully reprinted from
Hold hard, cobbers Vol. 1, Robin S. Corfield
© 1992, 57th/60th Battalion Association
Our thanks to Bill Gammage for his contribution to the
notes in this reprint.

Cover and map by Alex Snellgrove
Typeset by Gail MacCallum

Printed by McPherson's Printing Group

ISBN 1 875989 26 9

To
the memory of
those of my comrades
who rest on their arms, this
record of their sacrifice is dedicated.

CONTENTS

INTRODUCTION

William Downing

My father, Walter Hubert Downing ('Jimmy' to his friends), was born in 1893 at Portland in Victoria. He hated having his photo taken. Due to this, and because at different times both his house and mine were destroyed by fire, there are only a few photos of him in existence today. One of them is a family photo. His sister, my aunt Gwen, said they had got him up nicely when he disappeared. He got into a fight with some of his colleagues, so he appeared in the photo with a hastily smoothed-down collar and a very pugnacious look on his face.

As the youngest boy, he was rather spoilt by his sisters, and could be thoughtless. Gwen and Cath used to recall how he would hand them his creams to be washed, dried and pressed on the morning of the day he was to play in a cricket match. He went to Scotch College and then began to study law at Queens College, University of Melbourne. He won a University Blue in lacrosse and edited the Melbourne University student magazine.

When World War I broke out he tried to enlist, but he was too short and was rejected eight times, thereby missing Gallipoli. For the ninth occasion he had some friends hoist him up by the shoulders and weights were tied to his feet to stretch him. Then he was hurriedly measured, before he reverted to his usual height. He was found to be just tall enough and was finally enlisted on 30 September 1915.

Jimmy was put in the 7th Battalion of the Australian Imperial Forces (A.I.F.), and sent to Egypt for his final training. There he was offered a discharge because of a dislocation and cracked bone in his right arm, which he declined. He was transferred to the 57th Battalion, in which he served for the rest of the war. In mid-1916 he went into action in France, where he attained the rank of sergeant. He was offered a commission but turned it down, as that would have meant being separated from the men he had fought alongside. At Polygon Wood his platoon was advancing under cover of an artillery barrage, but the barrage fell short, and shells were exploding among his men. He calmed their panic and organised a retreat to a safer place. For his calm action in these circumstances he was awarded the Military Medal.

Three years of trench warfare took a heavy toll on his health, and in 1918 he applied for leave on medical grounds. He believed he had lost a great deal of weight, but one of the officers who considered his application rejected it with the comment: 'He was always a skinny little runt.' Fortunately, the war ended soon after this and he was able to take leave in Italy.

Jimmy had a Rowntree's chocolate advertisement, in the form of a scroll with a very impressive seal, which he had torn from a box. Whenever he got on a train in Italy, he would flash this scroll at the conductor, who would never look at it more closely, and so was able to travel to Rome without having to pay anything.

In Rome he enjoyed himself, and when the time came to return to his unit he decided to stay on and blame a nearby earthquake for his delayed return. But he was tipped off that he had been spotted by the authorities, and that in any case the earthquake story would not hold water. He needed to get back to his unit in France without going through passport control at the border. He travelled up from Rome with some French troops, one of whom kindly lent him parts of his uniform so he could line up and receive a wine ration, a benefit unknown in the Australian army. Just outside Milan, Jimmy left the train and 'borrowed' a baker's cart, pushing it into the city as a cover and abandoning it in the main square where its owner would be able to find it. He then travelled by foot and trams from village to village across northern Italy into Southern France, avoiding border check points and using his Rowntree scroll to 'pay' his fares.

But his unit wasn't where he had left it. In fact, it was no longer in France. Somehow Jimmy managed to hitch his way through France and across the English Channel, rejoining his unit in England. The paperwork was obligingly 'adjusted' and there was no fuss about his absence.

Back in Melbourne in 1919, he used his repatriation money to enrol at Queens and complete his law degree. After graduating in 1920, he opened a practice in partnership with a fellow student, Ted Williams, but this was soon dissolved and Jimmy joined his former divisional commander, Brigadier-General Harold 'Pompey' Elliott, to establish the firm of H.E. Elliott and Downing. In 1929 Jimmy married a beautiful young woman, Dorothy Louise Hambeleton, known to her friends and family as 'Pip'. They were lucky enough, because of the Depression, to be offered a large house at Ricketts Point for a peppercorn rent, and the three of us (this was soon after I was born in 1930) moved there. I acquired three younger brothers: James, John and David. We ran poultry in the grounds. My father's income diminished almost to nothing and we would swap eggs for the vegetables grown by unemployed men on some empty land at the back of the house.

Elliott had been under tremendous strain during the war and with the stress of the Depression he broke and committed suicide. The press was generally considerate — even the notorious Melbourne *Truth* — and simply reported that Elliott had died. The exception was *Smith's Weekly*, which blazed the headline 'General Elliott Commits Suicide'. This gave *Truth* the rare opportunity to be sanctimonious, and it published a slashing attack on *Smith's Weekly*, the 'so-called soldier's paper'. Years later, when one day I bought a copy of *Smith's*, father told me: 'If you want to waste your money, you can buy this paper. If you want to waste your time, you can read it. But don't bring it into this house!'

My father was in the militia and became a lieutenant-colonel before retiring in 1935. He was also an active member of Legacy.

At Ricketts Point we had a Dalmatian pup with a very loose skin, which drooped around his frame. He looked such a picture of misery that we called him 'Miz'. Soon enough, though, he grew to fill his hide, and was then a very handsome animal. One day he ran across the road in front of our local bus and was knocked down. The distraught driver carried him up to the house, where he was put to bed in the kitchen and fed warm milk laced with honey. Every night father would come home to Miz lying on his bed, whining in misery: 'Ooooh.' Father would pat and console poor Miz, and feed him his milk and honey.

'I'm worried about Miz,' he said to mother one night. 'He doesn't seem to be getting any better.'

'He's having you on. He's perfectly all right.'

'No ... can't you see how sick he is?'

Soon after this, father came home early one day and found Miz running around quite happily. But as soon as father's regular bus was heard on the road, Miz went into the kitchen, lay down on his bed, and started groaning in agony: 'Ooooh.'

'Why, the little fraud!'

Later, another solicitor joined my father and the firm became known as H.E. Elliott, Downing and Oldham. We moved from Ricketts Point and Miz was killed after falling over a cliff while trying to avoid a fight with another dog. My three brothers went down with polio during the epidemic.

My father published his first book, *Digger Dialects*, a collection of the printable slang used in the army, in 1919. He once told me he wrote it in a weekend and sold the rights for seven and sixpence. Some of the chapters in his second and last book, *To the Last Ridge*, appeared in the Melbourne *Herald* and the *Argus* before being published as a book in 1920. The publisher went to the wall at the time of publication, and my father received a great many copies of the book in lieu of royalties. These were later destroyed in a fire — there is only one copy of the original edition in our family.

To the Last Ridge essentially describes the sixteen battles in which the A.I.F. fought on the Western Front, in all of which my father was involved or on the fringe. The next year he won the Dublin Prize for this book. (This is a prize awarded by the University of Melbourne for achievements in the arts and sciences.) Perhaps the highest praise it received was in my father's obituary in Legacy's *Weekly Bulletin*: 'This book is considered by many to be the finest and most graphic description of these actions ever written from the point of view of the serving soldier.'

Although my father was modest, as this book shows, he took great pride in what he had done, and in those with whom he had been associated in France. He believed that we have a duty to help those less fortunate than ourselves and had a positive attitude towards life. One of his sayings was, 'Cast your bread upon the waters, and it will turn up buttered toast.'

He died on 30th October 1965.

William Downing
Melbourne
1998

PUBLISHERS' NOTE

The literary accounts of Australians at war are plentiful but thin. In his introduction to the 1920 edition of this book, Brigadier-General Harold 'Pompey' Elliott noted that few soldiers 'have the gift of literary expression, and for the most part their feelings remain a sealed book to those who come after; but here we do find them expressed.' Elliott recommended the book to the families and friends of those who had fought, and believed that *To the Last Ridge* provides 'the true picture — the monument we still want for our "rich dead" whose memory is ours and our children's great heritage.'

Walter Downing served in the 57th Battalion of the A.I.F., which was formed in Egypt on 21 February 1916. Half its men were Gallipoli veterans from the 5th Battalion, half fresh from Australia, like Walter. The 57th Battalion was in the 15th Brigade (commanded by Brigadier-General Elliott), which was part of the 5th Division. In early 1916 an Australian infantry battalion comprised about 1100 men; by mid 1918 many had only 150 men, and some had been disbanded.

When the Australians entered the trenches in northern France, the Western Front, that huge line of trenches running from the Belgian coast to the Swiss border, had been in existence for over eighteen months. The pattern had been established of a miserable stalemate interrupted by futile efforts by either side to break through each other's lines, accompanied by massive and horrific losses for the attackers. The trenches, barbed wire, and machine-guns made it a defender's war. The Australians arrived in time for the battles of the Somme, yet another futile and tragic series of assaults ordered by Sir Douglas Haig, the British commander-in-chief of the empire's armies.

What follows is an edited version of the first, 1920 edition of the book. Most changes are small, except for the deletion of the original, brief final chapter about the voyage home, and the moving of the original first chapter to the end of the book. The amount of explanatory material we could have provided was enormous, but we finally decided to keep notes and maps to a bare minimum. This book's great strength is in its portrayal of one man's localised and sometimes confused experience of battle, and to have provided too much of an overview of events would have detracted from this. Readers seeking this can turn, as we have done, to the admirable *Oxford Companion to Australian Military History* for a summary, or, for more detailed accounts, to R.S. Corfield's fascinating story of the 57th and 60th Battalions, *Hold hard, cobbers* (Vol.1), available from the bookshop of the War Memorial in Canberra, from where we have taken the lists of names of all who served in the 57th Battalion that form an appendix to this book.

All the names of individuals in *To the Last Ridge* are fictitious.

The Western Front ran from the Swiss border to the
North Sea, near which the Australians fought.

1

Fleurbaix, or Fromelles, was the A.I.F.'s first big battle in France. Downing's 5th Division and the British 61st Division attacked at night across boggy ground into heavy machine-gun and artillery fire. The Australians broke into the German front but the next morning were driven out. The 57th Battalion, in support, lost 35 men; the 5th Division lost 5,533. Fromelles was the most calamitous night in Australian history.

I

FLEURBAIX
19th July 1916

THERE IS a holy place by a little stream, a marsh between the orchards near Fromelles. This is its story.

From 10th to 17th of July the Black and Purple Battalions held the line. On the night of the 12th there was an alarm — the S.O.S. (two red stars hovering in the night) —, barrages, counter-barrages. There were raids and violent shelling. There was the frightful chaos of *minenwerfers* (trench mortars), shaking the ground into waves, trailing lines of sparks criss-crossed on the gloom, swerving just before they fell, confounding, dreadful, abhorred far more than shells, killing by their very concussion, destroying all within many yards. The enemy knew that a division fresh to the Western Front was in the line. He was bent on breaking its spirit. How little he succeeded, those battered breastworks and the little marsh bear witness.

No man's land, on the front occupied by the 15th

Brigade, was a double curve like the letter S. It was from five to seven hundred yards wide, narrowing on the left to two or three hundred, where the 8th and 14th Brigades were placed. At the wide end it was split lengthwise by a little stream, which wandered at last beneath our parapet by Pinney Avenue, where the tunnellers worked.

By the stream the ground was marshy but not impassable, for it was mid-summer. On either side, the British and the German lines fronted each other on low opposing slopes, rising in tiers — front line, supports, close reserves, reserves. Owing to the wet, low-lying nature of the ground there were no trenches, but solid breastworks of beaten sandbags reveted with iron and timber, fortified with concrete slabs or 'bursters'. These were from twenty to thirty feet thick, and seven to ten feet high. There was no parados (rear wall of a trench). A fire step was in every bay and a sandbag blockhouse used as a dugout.

Two miles behind our line was the village of Fleurbaix, occupied by civilians. Further back was the town of Sailly-sur-la-Lys. On the right, as one faced the front, was Laventie. Behind the German line was a large and lonely farm, and Fromelles, on a high ridge, where French and Indian cavalry fought in 1914. There was also that rising ground on the right named Sugarloaf. The graves of Englishmen lay everywhere; the dates on the little crosses had almost faded since 'December, 1914', 'February', 'May', 'October, 1915'. Most of the graves were nameless.

For several days trench stores, materials for the attack, picks, shovels, light bridges for the creek and scaling ladders were carried through the saps.

Through Brompton, Exeter, V.C., Pinneys and Mine Avenues they were carried by day — and held high. One could look into the white German communication saps meandering over the hillside. The Germans could look into ours.

The attack was to be made on the 17th. The objective was the German second line. The strategic reason was provided by the presence of a number of Prussian Guards divisions about to entrain from Lille to the Somme, and by the imminence of the important battle of Pozières. The British Army was numerically much weaker than the German, and subterfuges and diversions were necessary.

All this was known to pseudo-refugees, to spies, in the villages behind. Enemy airmen observed the white and coloured cloths spread in order and in designs in fields, like washing left to dry, according to the custom of the *blanchisseuses* (washer-women) of Flanders. Fields were ploughed lengthwise, crosswise and diagonally. White horses were depastured in particular fields. Even the genuine inhabitants knew far more about the attack than we. The Germans were in possession of a copy of operation orders before our battalion commanders had received them. And in those days information was not freely communicated to junior officers and the rank and file, as was afterwards the custom.

On the 17th July, within five minutes of zero time, the attack was countermanded.

On the 18th, the 59th and 60th took over the sector. The 57th were withdrawn to sleep for the night. We lay in a mill on the outskirts of Sailly, on the Sailly road. Sleep was sweet — for thousands it was their second last. Nevertheless, we neither knew nor cared what the morrow might bring. One accepts the immediate present, in the army. We woke with the birds, reminded of friendly magpies in the morning back in Australia. Here were only twitterings under the eaves, but at least it was a cheerful sound, pleasant on a lazy summer morning when the ripening corn was splashed with poppies, and the clover was pink, and the cornflowers blue under the hedges.

In Sailly, in the morning, we listened to the chatter in the *estaminets* (cafes). At the mill, old women and very small girls were selling gingerbread and sweets with cognac in them, sitting on stools, gossiping among themselves.

At midday we were told.

Usual preliminaries were gone through. Operation orders (including some indifferent prophesying) were explained, or as much of them as was thought fit. Rations and ammunition were issued.

At a quarter to two we moved off. Shelling commenced. These were the days of long and casual bombardments. Labourers were hoeing in the mangold fields. Stooping men and women watched us pass, without ceasing their work. It may have been courage, or stolidity, or the numbness of the peasant bound to the soil, or else necessity, that held the sad tenacious people here in such an hour of portent. Their old faces were inscrutable. They tilled the fields on the edge of the flames, under the arching trajectory of shells.

Bees hummed in the clear and drowsy sunshine. There was little smoke about the cottages, where the creepers were green. The road curved between grass which was like two green waves poised on either side.

We battalions came to the four crossroads where there were trenches in the corn, by a crucifix of wood in a damaged brick shrine. There was much gunfire. We waited.

Late in the afternoon we were ordered forward. From his crucifix the Man of Sorrows watched our going. One wondered if His mild look was bent especially on those marked for death that day. We left the road at an old orchard, and entered a sap (connecting trench). We passed V.C. House and wound down V.C. Avenue. Shells fell rapidly.

A bald man with a red moustache lay on a board, very still, his face to the wall. The sap was littered with rubbish, splintered wood and iron poking from the heaps of burnt earth. Here and there the sap was completely blown in. Then there were more dead. Further on, it was no sap, but a line of rubble heaps. We came to the Three-Hundred-Yard line. Then, issuing from a sally port, we dashed through the shrapnel barrage in artillery formation, and reached the front line. Again we waited.

A sad-faced man, sitting beside a body, said, 'Sniper — my brother — keep under the parapet.' Here the line was enfiladed (shot at) from the left flank where it curved.

The 59th and 60th were in the line. They knew their orders by heart. They were to wave their bayonets and cheer, then remain quiet. Three times this would be done. It was a bluff. They would not go over.

When this had been done once, the order to attack

7

ran from mouth to mouth. 'Over the bags in five minutes — over the bags in five minutes'; so it passed along. Then, 'Over you go.'

The 60th climbed on the parapet, heavily laden, dragging with them scaling ladders, light bridges, picks, shovels, and bags of bombs. There was wire to go through, and sinking ground; a creek to cross, more marsh and wire; then the German line.

Scores of stammering German machine-guns spluttered violently, drowning the noise of the cannonade. The air was thick with bullets, swishing in a flat lattice of death. There were gaps in the lines of men — wide ones, small ones. The survivors spread across the front, keeping the line straight. There was no hesitation, no recoil, no dropping of the unwounded into shellholes. The bullets skimmed low, from knee to groin, riddling the tumbling bodies before they touched the ground. Still the line kept on.

Hundreds were mown down in the flicker of an eyelid, like great rows of teeth knocked from a comb, but still the line went on, thinning and stretching. Wounded wriggled into shell holes or were hit again. Men were cut in two by streams of bullets. And still the line went on.

The 59th were watching from the breastwork.

Here one man alone, there two or three, walked unhurrying, with the mien of kings, rifles at the high port and tipped with that foot of steel which carries the spirit of an army — heads high, that few, to meet the death they scorned. No fury of battle but a determined calm bore them forward. Theirs was an unquestioning self-sacrifice that held back nothing. They died, all but one or two who walked through the fire by a miracle. A few had fallen behind in the marsh, exhausted by the weight they carried. Some had fallen in the creek, and under their heavy equipment could not mount the slippery banks. There were also some slightly wounded.

Fifty-six remained of a full thousand. It was over in five minutes.

And then the 59th rose, vengeful, with a shout — a thousand as one man. The chattering, metallic staccato of the tempest of hell burst in nickelled gusts. Sheaves and streams of bullets swept like whirling knives. There were many corpses hung inert on our wire, but the 59th surged forward, now in silence, more steadily, more precise than on parade. A few yards and there were but two hundred marching on. The rest lay in heaps and bloody swathes. They began firing at the German line as they advanced. Lewis gunners dropped into shell holes and fired burst after burst, dashing from cover to cover.

A hundred men broke into a wild but futile charge, determined to strike, if possible, one blow, but enemies pressed their red-hot thumbpieces with blistered fingers, spraying death from the tortured muzzles. That hundred lay flat in the attitudes of sleep.

It grew quiet again. A few wounded crawled in the grass, sniped at by riflemen. Then there was silence. Eighty came back that night.

Two companies from the 58th rose from the breastwork — the remainder were elsewhere carrying ammunition — and advanced by rushes, with covering fire. In banks of battle reek the sun went down, as red as blood.

As darkness drew on, the 57th went forward, but most were recalled almost before they left, for there was nothing to be gained by further loss of life. A few reached the creek.

It was the Charge of the Light Brigade once more, but more terrible, more hopeless — magnificent, but not war — a valley of death filled by somebody's blunder, or the horrid necessities of war.

The handful in our trenches stood to arms all night, because the line was now dangerously weak, for there were no supports and no reserves, and many enemy élite forces were in front.

The bays and traverses were jammed with dead and wounded lying head to foot for two miles, in a treble row, on the fire steps, beneath them, and behind the blockhouses. Wounded came crawling in, rolling over the parapet and sprawling to the bottom. A white-faced boy, naked to the waist, was being led along the trench, a hole in his side. He cracked some joke, then, 'I think I'll spell a minute; it's all going dark.' He sat down. An hour later someone shook him, but he was stiff and cold.

A barrage chopped and pounded on the crammed line. The blockhouses were packed with dying men. Men shot through the stomach screamed for water. In mercy it was denied them. Some pleaded to be shot. High explosive crumped in the line; shrapnel crashed in the air.

Out in front wounded were firing in a careless passion of rage, blazing at the inexorable parapet. This was stopped by a flurry of enemy fire. The interminable hours wore on. It was a night of horror and doubt. Parties went forth to rescue the wounded and to find whether any Australians were in the German trenches. Many more were hit. Wounded were calling for their

mates. There was a pause in the shelling. One in delirium was singing a marching song far out in front —
'My mother told me
That she would buy me
A rubber dollie,
A rubber dollie,
But when I told her
I loved a — '

On the left bombing was occurring. We heard the fragments wailing like Banshees in the air, and listened, thinking it was the cry of the wounded. A machine-gun rattled somewhere, and suddenly stopped —
'But when I told her
I loved a soldier, — '
The voice rose an octave —
'She would not buy me
A rub— '
There was another burst of fire and the singing ceased.

Someone cried continually, 'Bill, Bill,' all that night, but Bill did not answer. Between the salvos of shells we heard him again and again till dawn. Then that voice also was stilled.

A few of the 57th and 58th were engaged in rushing ammunition to the front line. All the rest were bringing in wounded. By dawn, in spite of strenuous labours, only half the wounded and a few of the dead had been brought in. For five nights this work was unremitting. Parties went out under fire in broad daylight. Some of the wounded were never found. A few crawled in three weeks later, with shattered limbs and maggoty wounds. They had hidden from our parties, fearful lest they might be Huns, swooning often, uncertain which was our trench and which the German, drinking putrid shellhole water, foraging by night for food among the dead, lying low by day.

All night the 8th and 14th Brigades were fighting for their lives, almost surrounded, up to their breasts in the water with which the enemy had flooded their trench. In the morning they extricated themselves with immense difficulty and heavy loss, and withdrew through saps rushed forward from our line by the Fifth Pioneers. The next night some, after wandering lost in enemy country, returned by immense good luck and after astounding adventures.

For three days hundreds of wounded lay uncom- plaining in their torment, in our line. The survivors were few by comparison with the dead. It was an hour's hard work for four men to carry one to safety. All joined in the task. The very safety of the line was imperilled by the number of men engaged in this merciful duty. We carried till the mind refused its task and limbs sagged, and always there were hundreds for whom each minute decreased the chances of life. Release came to very many of the stricken. We left the hopeless cases undisturbed for the sake of those whom the surgeons could save.

For days an officer, blind and demented, wandered near the German lines, never fired on, but used as a decoy to attract his friends to their death. These were shot while attempting to reach him. He wandered up and down the line till he died, avoiding friend and foe alike.

This charge received a recognition from the enemy which reasons of state denied from our own side. A noble act here lights up the murky record of the German army. Two gallant enemies carried a wounded Australian to our parapet, stood at the salute, then turned and walked away. They unfortunately neglected to secure a safe conduct, and were shot, to the sincere regret of every Australian there, by someone in the next bay, who, owing to the shape of the line and the direction they had come, was in ignorance of their errand.

The remnants of the 57th and 58th held the front line system for a further fifty days, making fifty-nine in all, without relief.

And the sandbags were splashed with red, and red were the firesteps, the duckboards, the bays. And the stench of stagnant pools of the blood of heroes is in our nostrils even now.

II

MUD
October to December 1916

WE CAME to Montauban. There was accommodation for about a hundred men in tents, but there was running water on the earthern floors. Seven hundred men shovelled the mud away and slept in the open. That night winter set in with bitterly cold rains.

Two months before, Montauban had been a battle-field. Where there had been a village, the searcher might find a few bricks, but these soon sank in the morass. The ground, apparently solid, was crumbly beneath the surface, as always where the iron storms have played. It was, therefore, easily churned to mud by the feet of men and mules and by wheels. The very metal of the roads was pressed below that deep engulfing tide. Owing to this, and to the congestion of the traffic, two-muled limbers (detachable front sections of gun carriages) were seven hours on the road from Mametz, three miles behind. Down Sausage Gully, up the farther side and over the hill by Bazentin we slipped and slid. We entered a waterlogged sap where one or two duckboards (planks laid over mud) were uselessly floating. Then there were no more duckboards but mire, to the thighs at best, to the middle at worst. There men were caught as in a vice. There were wires in which one's equipment caught fast. They wound about the sights of one's rifle, pulling its strap from one's shoulder, so that it fell in the ooze which covered the gripping clay, as one battled with one's legs. There were occasional bodies underneath, possibly of some lonely nightfarer who had been wounded and had struggled till he sank or, unconscious, was suffocated without a struggle, the manner of his end a secret of the bog. The effort of lifting one's rear leg clear, then pushing it forward, drove the other into deeper, more tenacious clay.

Somehow, the majority reached High Wood, where for a space the going was better, but where the shelling was heavier. Here a Scotchman and a German had lain for three weeks beside the communication trench, each impaled on the other's bayonet, witness to the severity of the fighting for those hills. In a shellhole a complete German machine-gun team were grouped around their gun, as if petrified in the attitudes of life — Number One, with his grey, grim face, firing his silent weapon; Number Two intently handling the belt; Number Three busied with the rusty boxes; the rest observing. We passed a monument to an entire English division.

For two miles through labyrinthine ways we moved to the firing line. We arrived by driblets, after many hours of toil, of utter exhaustion, and of irritating halts while parties of men, clogged, laden and bulky, pushed past us, and stretcher-bearers, with their burdens of pain, squeezed through the narrow sap. Stretcher-bearers had an awful time, and it was heartbreaking for everyone. All the time shells and rain fell from the leaden, pitiless skies. There was no avoiding the one or the other, either then or in the following days. What few dugouts there were were full of water. We were buried to the waist in clay and slush, which increased as the drizzle came steadily down.

The dead lay everywhere. The deeper one dug, the more bodies one exhumed. Hands and faces protruded from the slimy, toppling walls of trenches. Knees, shoulders and buttocks poked from the foul morass, as many as the pebbles of a brook. Here had been a heavy slaughter of English lads four days before; so great had been the price in blood and sweat and tears of those few acres. There were also German dead, but it was hard to tell them from the rest, for khaki is grey when soaked and muddy.

Our clothes, our very underclothing, were ponderous with the weight of half an inch of mud on the outer surface, and nearly as much on the inner. Casualties were heavy in the sixty hours we were in that place. The days were bad, but sixteen hours of a cold, pitchy night was a burden not easily to be borne. We were shot at from three sides, and it was torment. There was no hot food and no prospect of it. We drank shellhole water, as it was too cold for the corpses to rot. We were soaked from head to feet (the feet that were never dry all that winter) with sweat and icy mud.

We did not sleep, but waited in a torpor as the minutes crawled past. The old P.H. gas helmets — like the nosebag of a horse — were still in use, and cold on one's neck and face. We were mud to the eyes; our chilled fingers bled. Everything we touched was slimy; so were our hands; so also were our biscuits and our bully beef.

According to the newspapers, the enemy was running short of ammunition at this time. The sardonic comment of the men was that 'Fritz had given up making shells and was firing his foundries over.' The only dry things in that place were powder and wit.

On our immediate front was the Butte de Warlencourt. Beyond lay Bapaume. Both seemed inaccessible as the moon. On the former many bloody attacks were made, but always with indifferent success. Our task was to have been its capture. Fortunately at the end of our time we were judged too exhausted for the undertaking. That mound was never ours till the enemy retired in February after the freeze. Before being relieved, we pushed new trenches forward and captured a few Germans. Then we began the backward journey.

A greatcoat, wet and muddy, weighed forty pounds or more. Soaked equipment laden with one hundred and seventy rounds of ammunition and two or three bombs felt like the load of Atlas. The rifle-sling over the chest, when the rifle was carried diagonally across the back, strangled our panting breath. If hung from the shoulder, the strap repeatedly slipped to the forearm, the butt bumped awkwardly against the legs, and fell continually in the mud. At the most inconvenient moments rifles became entangled in the thousands of old telephone wires festooned across and along the trench in a mesh of tentacles which reached out and grasped the labouring men, became entangled in the equipment, knocked helmets in the slime, caught men under the chin and tripped their feet as they lifted them within the mud. The way was complicated by coils of barbed wire unwound beneath the surface of the slush, which tore flesh and clothes.

Short men fared particularly badly. Eight yards a minute would have been good going for a fresh, strong, unencumbered man. In a long line each one delayed the rest until he had mastered his individual difficulties. In every few yards there were places abnormally bad. Thus it frequently took a full hour for a hundred men to pass a given point. Parties met and jammed in the narrow saps. The bulging gear of each man scraped both sides of the trench at the one time. It was almost impossible for two men to pass.

Heavily laden, plastered with clay to the hair, with greatcoats dragging from their shoulders and trailing in the mud, tangled in wires, unimaginably weary, we struggled through the slough and through the night. It was dark as the unlit corridors of Eblis. Absolutely nothing could be seen except by the blinding flash of shells, the flicker in the sky of guns along the hills, the dazzling flares. These left baffling mirages of colour on the retina, preventing the eyes from becoming accustomed to the gloom.

Out of the saps and in the wide air men walked through the ground rather than over it. Nevertheless, there were in every few yards lumps of hard earth, slippery under a surface of slush. Stepping unawares on these, while the rear leg was held by the clay, the forward foot would slew round to an impossible angle, and toe pointing to toe, and both feet fast, men immediately lost their balance and fell into the shellholes at their feet, where the friable earth fastened on their bedraggled bodies. It was especially so when rubber thigh-boots were worn, for these had no grip of the ground. Falling, one's whole body was held as though by tentacles, and one rose only with labour. Many men habitually fell twice in five yards in the bad nights and the bad places.

We fell full length often. There was a foot of slush on the changing surface of the clay. The sound of the wrenching of our boots from its grip was like the tearing of sheets of cloth. We were weakened by hunger, shattered in nerve by the continued barrage. The rain poured in torrents. Our feet were swollen and frequently black with 'trench feet', and tingled in agony as the blood circulated once more through frozen toes. Some of us were forced to crawl. No matter how overcome, few dared rest. This was not on account of the shelling, which was severe, but because we might be unable to move again — might fall asleep and perish before morning.

We were often bogged and helpless. Artillery mules were used to drag us from the shellholes. Getting the mules out was a harder matter. Many had to be shot.

Companies took twenty-four hours, without halting for rest, to reach Montauban. The weaker men and those who had lost their way — an easy matter, for there were no landmarks — did not rejoin for days. Many who took the risk of sitting down found themselves unable to move, through cold, bad feet, exhaustion and weakness, till the next day brought succour. Torrents of frigid rain pelted down through all the black hours of night.

It was five miles to the camp, and there were no duckboards. It was mud, mud, mud all the way. Fire, land and water, Napoleon's other three elements, were ever present, but the fourth was the background of them all. Battalions were reduced to one sixth their strength by frostbite and trench feet.

In that dark winter the armies thought mud, ate mud, lived in a sea of hundreds of square miles of it. Europe failed many times to break the hearts of the men of the Antipodes, but was never nearer succeeding than then. But the hardy, alert and vigorous men of the Australian infantry, who, despite their reputation, are not heavy or big, battled through that eight months' agony (Flers in October to Bullecourt in May) in a morass. How we envied the airmen!

Men arrived in the line without gumboots (one of the means with which the authorities attempted to combat trench feet). These were generally four sizes too large, and were left deep in the first few yards of mud at the commencement of the weary battle with its grip all the way to the front line. Often men arrived minus socks and breeches, pulled from their legs in trying to wrench themselves from the morass with their hands. In this condition they had to remain deep in mud for four days, for the dearth of men was such that companies holding long fronts were down to a strength of forty or thirty or twenty men. The cold was bitter. Many were without greatcoats, rifles, equipment and Lewis guns, lost in the mire.

In the waterlogged trenches there were no dugouts, except sometimes in reserves, where an old German shaft might be pumped dry for battalion headquarters.

The duckboards reached rarely to within a mile of the front line.

Rations usually did not come. Ration parties lost their way or got hopelessly bogged. Sometimes they struggled around in circles all night, and dawn found them miles from their appointed place. Sometimes they all but wandered into the German lines. Many Germans were captured by wandering into our trenches, but there was scarcely one such case in the whole of the A.I.F. On one occasion a party was captured, bogged and lost in no man's land. Their German captors, equally bewildered, conducted them within our lines, and in their turn were taken.

On being relieved, the parties, six at a time, filed through the black night across the bog, crouching while machine-guns rattled and the bullets hummed past, standing like statues as the white and brilliant flares popped, then roared and curved, making the night like day, and fell and burned on the ground in white smoke. Then blackness, and on we struggled, feverish with anxiety to get away. At long length we reached the slippery duckboards that tipped beneath our feet and shot us into shell holes, with missing boards and great gaps where shells had blown the causeway to the winds. Now and again shells crashed in red flame and fragments whirred through the air. Artillery roared without ceasing, and there was a constant flicker in the sky, both over our artillery and over the German, which showed the black outlines of the hills in each recurring instant. We muttered as we stumbled over bodies, cursed as we dropped without warning into water. After hours we reached our camp, altogether pitiable, with bare feet puffed and cut by the duckboards, or swollen so that the boots had to be cut off them — weak and weary, caked with mud in various stages of drying, as in a cocoon — soaked, except our hands and faces — filthy from toes to hair — sometimes half naked. We came walking, or were carried on the backs of staggering mates. We rested a few days, were (possibly) given a bath, cleaned ourselves, and went back to the line.

III

A RAID

WE HAD our orders. We were at all costs to secure identification. A Prussian division had arrived from the Eastern Front (the part of Eastern Europe where Russia was fighting Germany and Austro-Hungary) and was somewhere in the line, probably opposite us. It had to be located or its presence disproved.

The trench mortars had been pounding the enemy all day and cutting his wire with Stokes and six-inch Newton shells. The heavy Newtons shattered his known machine-gun posts, the beautiful Stokes shot up and up and up in strings of ten and eleven, each humming like a blast on the bass notes of a mouth organ, and fell in successive crashes among the entanglements, splitting into long thin knives which could cut off a head as cleanly as a sword, or shear through thickets of strong wire. The Hun artillery replied with violence, then ceased.

Halfway across no man's land a telephone wire had been laid the night before, and the end looped back to our parapet. The signaller had only to go forward with the receiver and transmitter strapped to his head, while the Officer Commanding Operations directed the raid from our trench. But the latter, not being one in whom we confided, was left frantically to whisper his contradictory orders into an apparatus that was mute; for it had been seen to, with the connivance of the subalterns, that the wire was cut (broken by a shell, according to the report of that unsuspecting officer).

At night, having made certain of the conditions of success, we went forward in the faint moonlight, and lay in the snow. We waited. Our rifles seemed coated with glue, but it was merely the moisture on our fingers freezing on the surface of the wood.

We were wearing British uniforms, we were without badges, pay books, identity discs or letters. Our hands, arms, faces and necks were blackened in order to make them invisible in the night. The Prussians would be able to recognise Australians only by their handiwork.

Physically and mentally we were in splendid condition. We had been withdrawn from the line a week before for training, which consisted of bomb-throwing, bayonet fighting, boxing, football and obstacle races. Every man to the last private had an individual part to play. Two were stretcher-bearers; one was detailed to secure a tunic, and get away with it as quickly as possible; another was to lay a tape to guide the raiders back; others were to collect documents, weapons, stamped equipment or anything else which might interest intelligence staffs. Some were to go beyond the German line and protect the trench party from attack, and to cover the withdrawal; it was the duty of others to guard the flank and keep up machine-gun fire to the left and right of the portion of trench to be dealt with. There were knobkerry (club) men, bayonet men, pistol men and Lewis gunners.

We lay on our tapes.

The barrage came down on the enemy trench as though through a stencil, so perfect was the ranging. It lifted fifty yards, so we rose and followed it in a wave. We were fifty. A box barrage was being used, that is to say, four zones of beaten ground in the form of a hollow square, of which one side played at first on the enemy trench, and then a little beyond it, two lateral sides prevented aid for the garrison from coming from its neighbours, while the fourth worried the enemy supports. The only thing wrong with the barrage was that it did not leave enough meat for us.

In a few seconds we were through the remnants of the wire. Two greens shot into the air — the signal to the artillery that we were in the trench. The Huns on right and left were also firing flares, reds and greens and whites and tango yellows. Those in front of us never got much chance to fire anything.

There were cries of 'Share that among you,' as a shower of bombs fell in the trench. The appeal of 'Mercy, kamarad,' was dismissed with a curt 'No kamarad of mine, son!' or the sardonic, 'You're just two years too late.' Knobkerries and bayonets were hard at work. A cry was heard, 'No, no, Englander, I haaf seven kinder.' 'That's to make sure you won't have seven more.' Crash went a bomb (hand grenade) and *vmm-m-m* went the fragments.

Bombs accounted for all the Germans lurking in dugouts. A few of the enemy fought bravely, using their bayonets with a peculiar flourish and attempting to chop down on our heads, but we were always first, with a quick, straight point at throat or chest (not the stomach, for a man so transfixed grasps the blade). No living thing was left behind us in that trench.

A double red rocket was fired by the lieutenant. That meant 'Get back for your lives.' So we did, with a dozen prisoners. Men were exhibiting bloody bayonets and crying, 'I've christened the ——.' Others carried rifles with smashed butts which told their own tale. All were grinning through the blood and burnt cork that covered them. The whole thing had lasted ten minutes. Our casualties were two killed and a score of slightly wounded.

A double yellow flare was fired — 'All clear'. We made for the deep dugouts of the reserve line as fast as our legs would take us.

We were given a hot meal and rum. The prisoners got whisky, but that was to loosen their tongues when they reached the collecting depots.

That is all, except that the Officer Commanding Operations was given a decoration.

In February 1917 the Germans began to withdraw to the well-fortified Hindenburg Line. They covered their retreat with machine-gun fire, against which the Australians advanced for some four weeks.

IV

THE FREEZE
January and February 1917

IT BEGAN to freeze in December. At first a bitter misery of intense cold was added to the horror of the mud. Frostbite was rare, and trench feet, although no effective remedy had been discovered, claimed fewer victims than at first. This malady, worse almost than the worst wound, attacked the ball of the foot with a painful swelling which gave no rest for weeks, and with a black and spreading mortification which caused the loss of many a limb. The only preventive was friction, but hours of rubbing failed to restore the circulation to our chilled feet. It was almost impossible to massage them, for one was always knee-deep in mud, and had nowhere to sit down. Moreover one's hands themselves were plastered with filth, and there was nothing on which to wipe them, because everything else was equally muddy. At first whale oil, then camphor was used, but the only effective cure was a dry place to stand in. The authorities, alarmed at the wastage of personnel arising from this cause, attempted to meet the case by prescribing the following.

Trench feet was classed as S.I.W. — 'self-inflicted wound' (or 'somebody inflicted wound'). Divisional and all other commanders down to the harassed lance-corporal in charge of a section were threatened with the loss of their commands in the event of further cases developing, and all platoon commanders were ordered to furnish daily certificates affirming that they had personally superintended the foot-rubbing and had issued hot meals to their men, presumably conjuring the latter out of the air whenever none came to the line. Tins of solidified alcohol were issued, but these were seldom sufficient both to melt the ice and to boil the water, though even so much was an inestimable blessing.

At a point about a mile from the front trenches was a system of deep dugouts beside a quarry under a bluff, where the field kitchen used to cook meals for the line. It had the fantastic name of 'Miller's Son'. Here water was got from shellholes. Parties of men quarried the ice with picks, and brought it to the fire in bags. It frequently gave a weird taste to the tea, apart, of course from the usual flavour of petrol. Boiling tea and stew were poured into petrol tins which were bedded in kapok and feathers to keep them warm. But when these arrived in the line their contents were frequently frozen solid, even though there had been as little delay as possible in carrying them.

Late in January, 1917, it froze hard. There had been at first a crackling film of ice on the surface of the mud. It thickened gradually, and now there was no mud and no water, no slush of muddy snow. The great tanks at the water-points at Montauban and Fricourt were solid blocks. The mud plastered trees, the ground, the huts, the hills were like grey iron. There was rime on everything, except when melted by weak suns or washed by infrequent rain. The thermometer dropped slowly to twenty degrees of frost — some say twenty-nine, but we were already so numbed that it made little difference. It was the coldest winter in Europe for twenty years. But at least one could move about. Duckboard tracks and tramways were everywhere. They went even to the front trenches. A broad-gauge railway was built to Needle Trench, two and a half miles from the front line at Gueudecourt, zig-zagging over the hills with sublime impudence. The train puffed along every afternoon in the twilight, carrying supplies. Curiously, it was seldom shelled, and, for all I know, never hit.

Even by day, the bitter winds cut through greatcoats and sheepskins. One awoke at evening with one's clothes stiff as a board with frozen sweat. On one's blanket (if one were lucky enough to have a blanket), and on the lower part of one's face, the breath had condensed and formed a film of ice. One awoke at evening to another night of Herculean labours, of peril and misery, as the silent quest rose to a silent heaven, 'How long, O Lord?' from thousands of souls which had lost faith for a little in both their God and their country, from neither of which came aid. Some diary notes:

'Delville Wood, 26/1/17 — Just out of the line. Had a rough trot from shells. Some of our own stuff dropping short. Lobbed here at 3 a.m. yesterday morning. No blankets. Twenty-five deg. of frost. Feet aching. Can hardly bear to stand on them. Lousy from head to feet, and thoroughly miserable. Company's strength very low. Had four trips to the front line last night. First time with rations. Other three carrying duckboards, timber and sheets of thick iron for dugouts, and Stokes shells for a trench mortar barrage tomorrow night. Had to help Morgan with his load. Evans, Smith and Reid killed just in front of me. Shell lobbed among us just as we were picking up our loads; Evans and Reid killed outright. Smith wouldn't let us touch him. He scarcely stopped screaming till just before he died. Poor old Smithy, one of the best. McAlister had tinny luck. Got a piece in the leg and went off in a stretcher as happy as Larry. Duckboards covered with ice. Williams stopped a bit in the guts. He was very bad, and in great agony. Just as they were carting him off one of the stretcher-bearers slipped on the duckboards and fell with him.

'We had hardly got back to the dugout this morning when the major came around and roared up Sergeant Ellis for the tins and bits of paper lying round the trench. So we had to get out and pick them up. He'd been asleep last night when we were out. Then there was a rifle inspection and respirator drill. When we got it over we had to go on another fatigue.'

'27/1/17 — Three trips last night. No casualties. Pretty quiet. Blankets came. Feet too cold to sleep. Thought we were going out for a spell, but not. Bread four to one, but a good rum issue. No mail for six weeks now. Back to the line tomorrow. We just go into the line again and again until we get knocked. We'll never get out of this. Just in and out, in and out, and some-body stonkered every time. Australia has forgotten us, and so has God. I wouldn't wish my worst enemy to have to put up with this life. But we've got to go, and why shouldn't they too? All bound to get our "issue" sooner or later.'

'Ginchy, 2/2/17 — In the line and out again. It's a hopeless business.

"Tomorrow, and tomorrow, and tomorrow,
Crawls in this weary pace from day to day."

It's pitiable to see some of the men — utterly weary, but still battling on. No cases of trench feet this week, thank goodness.'

In places where boots might be taken off, they had to be thawed before they could be worn again. When in reserves, one went every night to the front line for work of some kind — ration-carrying for the garrison, building and repairing duckwalks, digging trenches and laying telephone cables. These fatigues were less arduous than in the season of mud, but more perilous, for flying ice and frozen earth were dangerous as steel.

Picks and shovels made no more effect on the ground than if it had been granite. The parties reached their work shortly after dusk. Engineers mapped out the ground to be dug and the infantry worked in a line of men often a mile long, standing like a thousand tinted statues while rockets slowly rose from the trenches, or parachute flares fluttered down, casting a brilliant light over all, staining the snow with different colours. Sometimes there was only machine-gun fire, sometimes we were caught in the barrage. At dawn, when the night had been normal, we returned by the duckwalks.

The duckboards were slippery with caked and frozen snow, and one's hamstrings grew sore and swollen through the unnatural strain of slipping backwards at every step, while carrying a heavy load. A hard lump of snow accumulated under the iron heelplate, so that one walked as though on French heels. The rough and frozen ground bruised our feet.

A ceaseless pressure on the enemy was maintained. Parties were sent out nightly to locate or capture enemy posts. Our patrols were continually encountering those of the enemy. There were fierce fights in the snow. Raids were frequent, and often assumed the proportions of a minor attack. If these were successful, as they usually were, they meant a large number of enemy casualties, the gaining of important information and the issue of decorations; if not — another string of bodies on the enemy's wire, and few decorations, if any: the principle being that the less said about them the better. The enemy seldom raided, not having much heart for the job; but when he did, the Australians invariably repelled him, wondering, with some bigotry, at his impudence in attempting to raid *them*. There were also minor attacks, such as that at Geuedecourt, with the object of straightening the lines.

As early as January we possessed aeroplane photographs of that system of trenches later known as the Hindenburg Line, and plans of the secret tunnels to its outworks. But what was probably the first definite information of the intended German withdrawal was gained from prisoners taken on the ninth of February in a raid by the 57th Battalion. They said that their army would be back in the 'Cambrai Line' by 25 March, and that a huge dump of our ammunition, covering several hundred acres between Montauban and Combles, would be bombed by airmen next morning. Both predictions were justified by the event. The dump was exploding and burning for thirty-six hours. The German soldier seems to have been trusted with an extraordinary amount of important information.

Early in March it began to thaw.

V

BAPAUME
March 1917

SINCE JANUARY the fourteenth we had been in the front line system. It was now the fourteenth of March. We were told that the Germans were about to retreat. We expected disappointment. Repeatedly since the middle of February our patrols had crawled to enemy trenches and found them deserted; but we knew that the German habitually conserved his garrison by such withdrawals, leaving only a few machine-gunners with a store of flares. He left his dugouts mined.

As a result we had succeeded in forcing him back, to a depth, in places, of three miles. But Bapaume, although a little nearer, and although still the lodestar of our hopes, seemed ever more remote. We tried to believe that some day we would be out of the mud, some day we would fight in the open. We tried to convince ourselves, and, in letters, those at home, that autumn would make an end; but the war seemed eternal. The Hun was still strong, still fighting well.

From local reserves in Pilgrim's Way, a sunken road on the right of Flers (of evil memory), we went past Fritz's Folly, a bank now sprouting green and covered with the grey and frozen bodies of British and

Australians, and of very many Germans. They bore witness in that place of the bitter fighting, to and fro. White skulls perforated with bullet holes lay here and there. We came by night to Barley Trench where the firing line fronted Beaulencourt and le Transloy, both on the right of Bapaume.

The enemy was six hundred yards away. A thousand yards beyond, with trees along it, was the main road through le Transloy from Bapaume. On the fringes of the former was a farm; on the outskirts of the latter, a sugar factory and a large concrete tank lying on its side. Both the village and the town were hidden by low hills, left and right.

A cloud of smoke hid half the sky by day. By night a red glow over the villages told its tale. There was fighting between our patrols and enemy outposts, and encounters in no man's land with strong parties of Germans. There were casualties on both sides, the enemy's were the heavier. His advanced positions all became known.

On the night of the fourteenth we formed in no man's land and approached the enemy's outposts by cautious degrees. They were vacant, so we went on. The enemy's wire was known to be extremely thick, and the artillery had not succeeded in cutting it. We were to get through as best we could, under cover of the confusion caused by throwing grenades into the trench. We arrived at the wire by twos and threes, without incident, crouching in shellholes when the Germans fired flares. We got among the wire. The Germans saw us and there was an exchange of grenades, but the trench was too far for good throwing — farther than we thought. The enemy opened fire with machine-guns while we struggled with the entanglements, tearing it with our hands. We could almost feel their flame. There were six of them within a hundred yards. Fortunately only about twelve out of seventy men were hit. The signal to retire was given. That proved difficult enough, for the Huns were sending up flares, and rattling on their machine-guns as though panic-stricken, or else very vindictive; but the business of getting our wounded back from the wire was much harder. Some were crying deliriously under the muzzles of the German rifles. Others groaned all the way back, drawing fire, though their rescuers held hands over their mouths. We got them all in, having sometimes to fight for them, except one. The Huns had him. He was one of only four men captured from our battalion during nearly three years' hard fighting in France.

The raid was not a success, as a raid, but it established that the enemy were still there in force.

On the next night we made another attempt, with the same result. At 4 a.m. on the morning of the seventeenth (St. Patrick's Day) we raided for the third time. Again we failed to penetrate the wire. By this time our total casualties were heavy. We did not think that that night we would sleep in Bapaume. At dawn a runner was passing from one post to another. Daylight came suddenly and the mist lifted. He noticed with surprise that he was not fired at. Growing bolder, he stood upright and walked across the shellholes. Soon men were moving over the whole landscape. It was a wonderful sight for one newly awakened from a brief sleep, whose mind was set in moulds imposed by the conditions of bog-warfare, to see from the front line men walking with impunity over the top.

Messages were sent to brigade headquarters; but by a few minutes the 58th battalion had beaten us for the honour of the first discovery. If we had raided an hour later than we did we would have caught the Huns moving out.

Our orders for the advance were to harry them on their way to the Hindenburg Line, and tumble them out of it before they got settled there. It was eight miles away. We passed the enemy's wire. It was deeper than we had known. We passed the trench into which we had three times failed to enter; and we looked curiously into it. We encountered a few German machine-guns, left, according to the enemy's custom, to bluff us into believing the main force still there, and ordered to extricate themselves as best they might after holding up our advance as long as possible. Their crews were killed or captured. We reached the Bapaume road with slight casualties, captured le Transloy and passed beyond it.

The 59th and 60th took up our task, passing through us where we lay in fields of rotting beet. Then there was a clatter on the road, the jingling of bits, as the cavalry came up. We had been with them in Fricourt Camp, lank Indians and tanned English. Far on the left, Australian Light Horse swooped round the corner of a wood, and were lost to view. Cavalry rode in groups through the straining battalions ahead, then opened in a wide line at a canter. They rode the German stragglers down. Machine-guns chattered as the horsemen galloped finely at them, but a man on a horse is hard to hit. We had never seen such things before. A riderless horse trotted back. Bayonets grouped and twinkled as the 59th and 60th flanked the enemy's posts, and converged in the final dash to his muzzles. Little groups of prisoners came towards us. Infantry and cavalry together encircled a village, then we lost sight of both. We marched into Bapaume. It was noon.

Early that morning patrols from the 6th Brigade, to the left of our division, had gone a little way into Bapaume, but had been blocked. About the same time the 8th, between the 6th and 15th Brigades, swept through the streets, now walking boldly, now fighting in the burning houses. The 2nd Division was fighting through the villages on the left of the town, as far as Lagnicourt and Noreuil, where it was stopped.

The ground was firm beneath our feet. Lord, the contrast! The hills were green. It seemed years since we had seen a pasture. Looking across the Slough of Despond, which stretched for twenty miles, back to Albert Church, the country fell away in steps, from Bapaume. Always we had thought we were before 'the last ridge', till the phrase became a catchword and a mockery, as later at Ypres.

One phase was past. We would meet the mud again at Passchendaele and Messines, but it would never be so bad; deeper, sometimes; colder, never; and never again so tenacious. Trees lay across the road outside Bapaume. The orchards were all destroyed. We were billeted in the town, in a smoking ruin. Every house had been utterly wrecked. The streets were choked with rubble. We wandered among the houses; we entered the vaults of the church, full of the skulls of centuries of monks; we went into the town hall, doomed to be blown up by a mine a week later. In the square the bronze statue of General Faidherbe had been taken away. There was a dummy anti-aircraft gun on its pedestal — a length of stovepipe. The town was nearly two miles from end to end. It must have been a pleasant place in times of peace. The railway lines were cut and curled by explosions. Outside the town, all the cross-roads were yawning craters, dangerous even to pedestrians by night. Here mines had been sprung to stop our transport. There were many belts of wire, to delay our advance and to hamper cavalry.

A motor lorry carrying a German aeroplane, with a red head and skulls and cross-bones painted on different parts of its body, entered the square. It had belonged to Prince Frederick of Prussia. A British airman had forced him to land between a German and an Australian post. Prince Frederick ran toward our men, then, seeing who we were, turned to the Germans; but he was mortally wounded by rifle fire, and was captured by a Light Horseman. It is curious that the only royal persons captured in this war were taken by Australians — one on the *Emden*, a German cruiser destroyed by HMAS *Sydney* in 1914, the other here.

VI

TRENCH MYTHOLOGY

I F ONE were to say that, in order to lift his mind from the crowding horrors of the day and night, and to relieve his monotonous hours, the Australian soldier sat in his trench and told himself fairy tales, he himself would indignantly deny it. Yet some of us did actually people the darkness and the mysterious land behind those low footbeaten mounds, which were all we saw by daylight of the German lines, with figures of phantasy. There is a strange fascination about the inaccessible. Men were prone to make themselves pictures, morbid and dark as the nightmares of Poe — pictures full of grotesque and humorous ogres. And these were men who, except in the matter of telling tales to the quartermaster or the brigadier, would never be suspected of imaginative gifts.

It was, of course, quite natural, if we were having a bad time, to wonder if the enemy were having a bad time also. From these thoughts the mind passed on to wonder what the normal existence of the enemy was like. Their infantry, at least (one thought), were pretty much the same as us, subject to the same miseries, the same annoyances and petty injustice of a soldier's life, 'hurt with the same weapons, subject to the same diseases, healed by the same means, warmed and cooled by the same winter and summer'. A fanciful curiosity led one to speculate whether the German also was lying on a ledge in the wall of a trench, covered with a waterproof sheet which could defy the drizzling rain, but could not prevent water from trickling down the trench-side until one was wet to the skin. We wondered of what kind were the homes they thought of, and their folk; one desired to be acquainted with the individual.

When we were informed that two Russian Poles, secret service men, were coming from the enemy lines, we watched them with envious wonder as they muttered in a dugout, after tumbling on us out of the dark, out of a fabulous country. With what momentous knowledge were they filled? To them those things were commonplace. Theirs was a vivid adventurous life, not a living death like ours. When we heard tales from an airman who came and went nightly between his aerodrome and a deserted moor in the heart of Germany, carrying our spies, who sometimes did not return, we wished for the romance of his existence; yet he did not know our moments of triumph, or the fierce ecstasy of the charge.

For how many was that phantom machine-gunner, of which every sector had one, 'Parapet Joe', a real thing? I knew a man — he had probably never heard of the horrible blind old man in Treasure Island — who used almost seriously to describe the Flare King, the old 'caretaker' of the German trenches as 'a square-built, stumpy old bloke', with only one watery blue eye, a wooden leg and a bushy red beard. His leg went tap, tap, tap around the trenches. 'That's the sound that sometimes you think is the enemy driving in stakes, when they're putting up entanglements.' Sometimes his leg slips between the grating of the duckboards. 'Then he foams at the mouth and curses outrageous.' There was the Minenwerfer Man, also a bogey — a big man with a heavy black beard that covered all his face except his little piggy eyes and the tip of his nose. He had a very wicked, ugly look. He had a cork arm with a hook on the end. These details of mutilation were probably reflexes, half-unconscious and dimly ironic, of the tales we had heard about declining enemy manpower. His wife lived in Berlin and sent abusive letters. He vented his irritation on us. His offsider was a tall, thin, fair young man with a hare lip and a cleft palate. 'He was always having rows with his boss.'

This man used to come to my dugout and give me detailed and circumstantial accounts of all the gossip of these queer phantoms. Yet his was not a dreamy nature. He was the best-humoured outlaw of the best-natured platoon of wild men that I have ever had the luck to know.

'Got a fag? Thanks. The Flare King's missus has got a job. Hear about it? In a corpse factory, on the mincer. Sent him a parcel this morning. Paper bed-socks and potted dog. While he was out giving old Minnies a hand to drop those werfers on Number Five post, the Minnie King's offsider ate the potted dog. Then the Flare Bloke came back, and had a box-on with him. Nearly gouged his eyes out. Squeal! No, that wasn't the brakes on the trolley behind his line,' (the generic German was always *he*), 'it was the offsider squealing — ' and so on.

One night there was a raid. While the raiders were waiting in our trench I heard him giving instructions to one of his cronies, 'Look out for the Flare King, and if you see him, knock him. He nearly got me knocked last night. He's a square-built bloke with — '

And he almost believed it.

VII

BEAUMETZ & LAGNICOURT
23rd to 26th March 1917

AFTER BAPAUME the course of the war entered a Golden Age of Australian arms, a brief sunburst of glory which ended in the gloomy battleclouds of Bullecourt.

In France the Australians had seen three main phases of the war. There was the introductory experience of quiet sectors at Ypres and Armentières where little of importance took place except raids and the artillery 'strafes'; next, we passed through a brief but bloody period of savage fighting, such as made sinister the names of Fleurbaix, of Pozieres and Mouquet Farm; third came the sordid drama of the Somme winter — equal to Gallipoli itself in hardship and disease, in duration, in unremitting strain, and possibly in bloodshed. And now for the first time in the war (excepting only the first few days of the landing at Anzac) came, for us, the days of open fighting.

It is easy to forget that until this time the mettle of our men had been tested only between parados and parapet, or in the short expensive rushes from trench to trench under heavy fire which characterised the previous periods, both on Gallipoli and in France. Consequently there was some fear lest the weary months of trench warfare should have resulted in a deadening of our offensive spirit, a diminution of our initiative. Nevertheless the qualities which had then been manifested made it probable that our men would easily adapt themselves to the new conditions; and it was even so. For the Australian is at his best when the day is disputed above ground, where his marksmanship, his cunning and his dash are allowed full scope; and when, having cleared a path with the bullet, he can see the result of his work, and the battle is decided by his favourite weapon, the bayonet. Then, not hampered by the horror of blind and soulless artillery, against which no man can fight, for him the prayer of Ajax is answered, and he 'sees his enemy's face'.

On the left of the Australian sector the 2nd Division fought forward from Bapaume through Beugnatre and Vaulx to Noreuil and Lagnicourt. There were many little 'stunts' around villages and sunken roads. Most of the villages were burning. One battalion in its advance had lost touch with the enemy. At nightfall there was before it a glare in the sky. The men went forward until at length they saw the doorways and windows of a village, lit with a red and eerie light — saw sparks from smouldering beams sailing in the wind. They approached without care, for a burning village was necessarily empty of Germans.

Then a bugle blew; and the village disappeared like a candle blown out, a magic palace of the Arabian Nights, transported away — all swallowed up in night. A hurricane of machine-gun fire roared from the outhouses, and our men, completely surprised, went down in scores; and in the darkness the survivors crawled into hollows and holes in the ground. The enemy, by an ingenious arrangement of lights and burning chemicals, had simulated the flames.

By day and by night the advance went on. The first attempt to drive the Huns from Lagnicourt was undertaken by two companies, and failed. Nevertheless, on the left the Hindenburg Line was reached. In the centre our men fought over the bare hills around Morchies, and ultimately that place was taken by the 59th Battalion. On the Australian right, between Morchies and the dark edge of Velu Wood (where the British were placed) the 15th Brigade trickled along sunken roads, and crawled through crops until the long and narrow town of Lebucquiere, lying among its hedges and its wheatfields, was encircled; and the men surged through the main street, driving the Huns before them, while the Light Horse rode over the slopes on the right. On Beaumetz-les-Cambrai, seven hundred yards beyond Lebucquiere, an attack was delivered without delay, and the same Germans who had lost the latter were driven from street to street, bombed from their ditches, sniped from house-tops as they ran. The 8th Brigade was fighting on the left.

Beaumetz was now a deep wedge within the German positions. In the small hours of the morning of the 26th of March, the second day after its capture, a heavy and determined attack was made on the village, then held by the 57th.

First came sixty *stürm-truppen*, picked men from crack regiments of Prussian Guards, all volunteers for the work, averaging six feet in height, clad in new uniforms of a beautiful blue-gray cloth and breeches of cord; with polished boots and patches of green suede leather on knees and elbows. Their faces were ruddy and shaven, their lips full-blooded, contrasting strongly with our men, who had not had a bath for weeks and on whose old, old faces and sunken cheeks was the stubble of days. These Prussians had been for three months in Germany in special training and on a liberal diet. Their business was to sweep our outposts from the path of the strong regiment following them.

A few German 77 millimetre shells were crashing in the outlying gardens. The night was pitch dark. A platoon of twenty men was holding an advanced post about a hundred yards forward from the village. Suddenly the sentries saw a line of figures, vague and gigantic in the gloom. There were whispered orders, and every man stood tensely at his post. A Lewis-gunner in an isolated section of the trench silently brought the butt of his gun to his shoulder, softly pulled back the cocking handle, took careful aim and pressed the trigger, startling the night with a loud metallic rattling. Ten shots, perhaps, had whirled from the pan into the breech, when the gun on which the lives of every man in that place largely depended became jammed. The Germans were now within sixty yards. Except for their rifles and revolvers, the four men of that machine-gun section were defenceless, but they stuck to their posts while the man on the gun took it to pieces, found the cause of the trouble, changed a damaged bolt for a new one; then, with hands that moved as fast as a pianist's, he assembled the gun by sense of touch alone, pushed home the piston rod, adjusted the body cover, snapped pinion and pistol-grip together, wound the return-spring, and had the gun once more in action, just as the enemy were upon him — just in the nick of time.

There ensued a fierce fight. Physically outclassed, weary and outnumbered by three to one, that handful fought till their enemy was exterminated, leaving only two or three prisoners. Meanwhile, on the outskirts of the town where three hundred and fifty men were holding a line in sunken roads and outhouses, we heard a machine-gun rattle and stop. Then, from the direction of the outpost came a splutter of musketry, an outcry, bursting bombs, shrieks and shouts of 'Hoch, hoch!' yells, cheers and curses. A runner with a gash in his face stumbled out of the darkness, gasped the password, stammered in his excitement, 'The outpost's being attacked.'

We ran forward to give our aid. We reached the outpost and were greeted with the news that the Huns had been wiped out. Some of the men were hilarious, others were silent. We sent the prisoners to the rear. Suddenly there was a cry, 'They're coming, they're coming! Man your posts.' A dense line of coal-scuttle-helmeted figures loomed out of the darkness. We fired and fired until the iron-work of our rifles burnt our hands. A runner from the rear came scrambling in. 'The whole line is being attacked. Retire to the village.' We hurried along a sunken road to the houses on the fringe of Beaumetz. Two or three minutes later we saw the Germans again, for it was nearly dawn. They were in three waves, about twelve hundred of them.

We shot the Huns as they came. In one place where they had broken in, there was wild fighting in the streets. Some of their snipers found shelter in a farm house two hundred yards on the left, and took a heavy toll of our men. There was a desperate struggle on the edge of the village, over the dawn and through hours of a sunny morning. Our men stood like iron. The fight swayed to and fro. At about eight in the morning the enemy retired, leaving very many dead, and all grew quiet again.

The fighting was of this nature all along the Australian front. On the afternoon of the same day an attack, in which some of the defenders of Beaumetz took part, was undertaken on the left, extending from the right of Morchies to Lagnicourt and beyond.

Advancing almost entirely without artillery support, our men swept over the hillsides in a long line, marching steadily, pausing only when blown over by the blast of bursting shells, or in order to drop on one knee to fire at the retiring enemy — shot at by machine-guns, advancing from sunken road to sunken road, bombing their way, fighting forward along the whole line.

German batteries were firing point-blank from the tops of hills at the oncoming waves. The German infantry retired from position to position, in some places fighting all the way; in others we could barely see their heads as they retired along trenches half a mile away.

When our men came close to isolated German batteries, the guns limbered up, withdrew a few hundred yards, blazed at the inexorable waves, and withdrew again. This continued till nightfall. Around one gun in particular there was some hot fighting. Some men, pushing beyond their objective, drove the gunners from the gunpit, and while attempting to run the gun out before dragging it away were counter-attacked and forced to return to our new line without it.

Meanwhile the left was prevented from advancing beyond Lagnicourt itself by the machine-guns and the barbed wire of the Hindenburg Line.

That night further objectives were taken, and we were able to consolidate our positions. In front of Beaumetz some German outposts established by the enemy during the previous night were rushed and captured. Some of the men who carried out this work had been involved in the fight that morning, had marched three miles in order to take part in the battle of Lagnicourt during the afternoon, had returned to Beaumetz and gone into the line, and had now taken part in the third operation of that day.

After a pause of a day, the 14th Brigade passed through the 15th (at Morchies and Beaumetz) and reached and stormed in turn Hermies, Boursies and Doignies, coming within sight of the chief defences of Cambrai, Moeuvres and Bourlon Wood, later to be the stage on which the English played one of the most moving dramas of their history.

The first phase of Lagnicourt had been the attack of the two companies; the second had been the general battle of March the 26th; the third took place a little later, when the 1st Division was attacked near that village. The enemy surged through a gap cut in his wire, and drove a wedge into our lines. The Australians, instead of meeting the main German force head to head, counter-attacked on the side of that wedge, and forced the enemy to retire through a narrowing gap to their own territory. But at the point towards which they were then shepherded by our men, the German wire was both thick and continuous. The Huns were therefore driven against their own impenetrable entanglement in the open, in broad daylight. There was a horrible scene as the Australians grimly pumped bullets as fast as they could work their bolts into a mass of Germans demented with terror, running to and fro along the front, screaming and screaming. It was a target that was impossible to miss — two or three hundred yards from our line. And the Australians did not pause until practically the whole of the German force lay in writhing heaps on the blood-sodden grass, and until these heaps were quietened by an unremitting stream of bullets.

And so the Hindenburg Line was reached along the whole front, and the forces dug in deeper and deeper. The open fighting ended, and we began a further phase of trench warfare, bloodier than ever.

Once the Hindenburg Line was reached an allied attack was planned. The British 62nd Division was to attack Bullecourt village, the Australian 4th Division the Line east of it. Without artillery support the 4th Division broke into the Line, a feat thought impossible, but then was driven out, suffering over 3,000 casualties. On 3 May the 2nd Division again attacked east of Bullecourt as part of a general offensive, and alone along the battlefront broke into the Line, and by bitter fighting extended its hold. On 8 May the 5th Division relieved it, and in a savage 'killing match' slowly advanced, until on 16 May the Germans abandoned the Bullecourt area.

VIII

BULLECOURT
April and May 1917

THE HISTORY of the last two years of the war in the west is, with interludes, the history of the Hindenburg Line, that mighty system whose great component lines bore names like Wotan and Siegfried. In three great festoons of many dozen parallel trenches, it ran from the sea to the Argonne woods. It was heavily wired, with belt on belt of high entanglements scores of yards in width. Through strong natural positions it followed the trend of the terrain. There was no foot of ground within a mile of it which could not be swept by its machine-guns.

The parallel trenches were connected by oblique 'switch' lines, like swinging gates; so that wherever any breach might be made the assailants would inevitably find themselves trapped in a deadly salient; and at each intersection of trenches there were places heavily fortified, villages and woods — Oppy, Quéant and the rest.

Quéant was the centre of an almost impregnable

knot of trenches in a vital strategic position. Two hundred thousand lives by the computations both of the enemy and of the allies would have been the price of its capture in a frontal attack. Hence it was decided by the High Command to undertake an encircling movement similar to that by which Combles had fallen into our hands the previous year; and that movement began with an attack on Bullecourt, a number of miles on the right flank of Croisilles.

And so, while a heavy pressure was maintained on the whole line from Vimy to St. Quentin, Australian divisions were flung one after another against the German army, in the hope of bursting through the succeeding fortified lines and exposing the flanks of the main position at Quéant, and of rolling up the German army from Cambrai to the sea. That project failed, but not for want of Australian effort or of Australian blood.

First, without artillery, but in company with twelve tanks, the 4th Australian Division was hurled at the enemy. The 4th Brigade and half the 12th, in rising from the ground, were met by a heavy barrage which immediately blew their ordered waves to apparently ineffectual human spray, and which at the same time shattered all but two of the tanks. Nevertheless, those two tanks and all the surviving infantry moved steadily forward in the broadening daylight under a heavy hail of bullets from the German trenches. They picked their way through the uncut entanglements (leaving many bodies hanging horribly on the wires) and reached the deep front trench, where in heavy fighting many Germans were slain. As soon, however, as the advance was continued, the two remaining tanks were both destroyed by concentrated fire from the German batteries. Undismayed, the infantry went on, fighting like wild cats every inch of the way — along trenches, across broad stretches of open ground, through wire and along the streets of Bullecourt, till they reached even to Riencourt on its rising ground.

Meanwhile the enemy had been pushing from the flanks and had succeeded in getting behind the greater part of these six battalions, and had so seriously threatened the rear of the remainder that the latter were forced to cut a passage back by the way they had come, sometimes in hand-to-hand fighting, with bomb and bayonet, and sometimes under a terrible storm of bullets.

And while these men, ignorant of the dire necessity of the rest, were engaged in extricating themselves from a hopeless situation, the Germans were surrounding their comrades with masses that grew denser and denser every minute. The devoted Australians had by now fired every cartridge, expended every bomb. They had nothing but their empty rifles and their bayonets with which to fight; and the enemy, seeing this, stood away and poured torrents of lead into the trenches where the poor remnants which had survived the previous fighting had taken refuge. Then, coming closer, the Germans began throwing bombs among our defenceless men who were still too stiff-necked to surrender. It was not long before it was evident that there was no hope of rescue and no means of escape; so by twos and threes the survivors, most of whom were covered with wounds, were taken.

Some of the captured men were then placed in trenches while the enemy, with a horrible deliberation, blew them to pieces with bombs. The rest were led away to suffer months of acute misery in German prison hells.

With this bloody disaster began a struggle to which Lone Pine, Verdun and Passchendaele alone are comparable: a battle which raged to and fro for five weeks, over a few square miles of ground, ceaseless, unrelieved in its horror, unsurpassed in the quantity and degree of the human agony, the sacrifice, the gallantry displayed; a battle whose fury is unsurpassed in the history of war.

Bullecourt represents for Australians a greater sum of sorrow and of honour than any other place in the world. The 4th Division went in and was all but annihilated. The 2nd Division went in, and in shattering the German hosts shattered itself. The 1st Division fought forward, and after a series of terrible struggles, left half its infantry on the field. The 5th Division took its stand on those terrible acres and won the last few yards that made Bullecourt ours, consummating, at a heavy price, the battles of the others.

Against the black horror of bitter sacrifice that was Bullecourt, a thousand gallant deeds shine forth. One could speak of the 2nd Division, which repulsed eighteen attacks in twenty-four hours — of the 6th Brigade, which, though surrounded and with three-quarters of its number wounded or killed, fought back-to-back for hours, until all the Germans who remained lay dead in heaps — of the 1st Division, smothered with barrages, sprayed with bullets, sunk in the mud, fighting from trench to trench, day in and day out, and both in attack and in counter-attack retrieving the fortunes of many a hard-fought battle — of the men of the 54th Battalion who, attacked by nine waves of Huns, fired their rifles till their enemies lay dead in swathes to the very lip of their trench, till their ammunition was all expended, and from the battle reek arose a fresh series of German waves; of the glorious and quixotic charge that our men immediately made, when, defenceless except for their bayonets, they sprang from the trench, two hundred of them, and walked towards the enemy, who believed them to be about to surrender, so few did the Australians appear; but our men broke into a run and charged and routed the Germans, who were to them as twenty men to one — and of the final capture of the village, in desperate fighting, by the 58th.

The ground was hideous with its dead. There were many times more Germans than Australians rotting in the shell-holes and the trenches: nevertheless the latter lay in thousands. Night and day a fearful barrage, the heaviest ever known to that time, played on our trenches and on the T-shaped saps we had dug forward into no man's land, in order to escape those death traps, our trenches; because the enemy artillery had the exact range of all his old lines.

Night and day our shells crashed and pounded on the Germans. It was a place of terror and of pity. The enemy fired shells at single men as they hurried to and fro across the ridge behind us, and even at stretcher-bearers carrying wounded men.

The best troops of the German Empire were flung into a battle that scarcely slackened at any time, even by a little, as long as the Australians were there. At last picked divisions from the Eastern Front, the Kaiser's personal bodyguard, the famous 'Cockchafers' themselves, were hurled into the battle, only to be shattered like the rest against a wall of indomitable infantry which seemed to grow more and more steadfast as it became thinner and thinner. Those Prussians bore the personal orders of their Emperor, 'I call upon you now, my Cockchafers, to meet an enemy more brave, more resolute, more hardy than any you have yet seen. I call upon you to defeat them.' They did not.

There was incessant fighting backwards and forwards, night and day. There were attacks, and counter-attacks by the Australians. Waves of Germans beat remorselessly on the defences they themselves had made. Those deep trenches were rocked continually by the concussions of a rain of heavy shells, and over the whole of the forward area every living thing seemed blotted out by the intensity of the barrage. One heard men squealing like trapped rabbits. One prayed for a little respite from the barrage.

Day by day the worn and white-faced ghosts of men dragged themselves from under the heaps of burnt clods that were flung by shellbursts into their trenches, and wiped the shattered flesh of comrades from their faces. The finest soldiers of two great nations came together in that charnel house; were slaughtered in thousands; riddled by bullets; rent, mangled, twisted and tortured by shells; suffered thirst, hunger, the heat of striving in battle at noon, the horror of dreadful nights, the frigid misery and the weariness of soul at daybreak; the torments of hell under fire; wounds; the loss of brothers and comrades; the frightful sounds and sights of death and agony; the nausea, the unutterable suffering of mind and soul and body that comes from the frequent tension of waiting to attack, and from nervous strain, long and unrelieved; the noise, the wailing, the silences — till life was hell.

This lasted for five weeks. There were trenches where the struggle never ceased, where bomb fights raged for hours of every day. These trenches were filled with corpses, over which men trampled and stumbled and fought like demons until the enemy were driven back a few yards and we could make a sandbag 'block' in the trench. And then the enemy would come again in force and drive us away; and so it would go on, now one side, now the other driving along the trench until its men and its strength and its bombs were exhausted, and then being driven back in turn.

Scraps of shattered bodies obtruded from the obscene earth. The country became more and more abominable, more and more desolate. Steel helmets, rusted rifles, parts of equipment, broken iron stakes, lengths of barbed wire were mingled in the tormented soil. The land was bare, except for stumps of trees, except for the railway lines, whose rails were broken and twisted and curled in a thousand places, except for houses of which only a shattered chimney or a broken wall remained.

With springing step, the light of youth in their eyes, one brigade after another, our men went into the line in battalions of six hundred. Dull-eyed, shambling, half-crazed, the wrecked battalions came out, after four days or a week, two hundred strong or less. Our artillery also suffered terribly, for it was at Bullecourt that counter-battery fire was first developed.

Recollections of Bullecourt are confused and horrible. Doubling through a ravine, full of shattered limbers and guns, torn equipment, disembowelled mules and dead men, full of the noise and the stink of bursting shells, full of flying lumps of red-hot steel, burring and whizzing and whining — sweating as we wound through a battered trench, cringing and recoiling as the shells burst almost in our faces, we came to a place where a white-faced officer with a streak of blood on his brow sat under a bank of earth, directing the incoming men.

One caught fragments of speech from someone in front, talking over his shoulder as he hurried forward, 'The boys are having a bad time — Boches trickling through.' 'Keep straight on, lads.' Stretcher-bearers worked like demons, sweating and panting as they stumbled over the rough ground with their limp and moaning burdens. Batteries of field-guns flashed and slammed behind us. The sky was lit in the east with the flare and flicker of the German artillery. It was a place where every sight, every sound, meant death — the screams of someone dying in agony, the monstrous clash and rumble of the guns, flinging hundreds of tons of shells each minute on our line, the swish of bullets, the pop of gas shells. There was nothing that was not ugly, distorted and horrible — nothing but the heroism of flesh contending with steel, and the flares in their diabolical beauty, filling with light that place of terror, so that German machine-gunners, strapped to their guns and straining their eyes as they sought a target in the night, might fill the hillsides with another kind of death.

We passed a Tommy lying on the ground. He was hatless. Part of his scalp was crinkled under the bloody hair, showing inches of the red skull; the fingers of one hand were smashed to pulp, the bloody putties were twisted on his broken legs, and he was moaning, 'Keep to the left, keep to the left, they want you there, boys, keep to the left.' We filed through communication trenches and reached the front line, leaving many of our number lying on the track. A man with both eyeballs hanging like poached eggs on his cheeks was sitting at the bottom of the trench groaning. Someone on the parapet was babbling in delirium. A couple of slightly wounded German prisoners were being led along the trench, stepping over the dead bodies, both German and Australian, that filled the bottom. There were cries on every side, heard in the pauses of the shelling. Gradually the barrage increased to a hellish intensity. There were shouts from the left, and the unmistakable sound of bursting bombs. The Huns were coming. Suddenly, in the half light (for it was now the dawn), we saw them. They seemed to rise from the ground, like Jason's earth-born warriors, begotten of dragons' teeth. We fired and fired our rifles till the iron burnt our hands and the grey masses sank once more from view, and for a little while the shelling slackened.

At dawn the troops on our left attacked, and all that day and all the next, we endured the barrage as best we might. On the fourth day there was a gas projector bombardment of the German lines. Short iron pipes were sunk in the ground, and their bases connected with an insulated wire. The pipes were filled with explosives and iron cylinders full of volatile fluid were placed in the mouths. Then when everything was ready an officer pressed a button, there was a violent roar, a long line of spearlike flames, hundreds of tumbling specks in the sky, and a cloud of gas smoke over the German line. The fury of the barrage redoubled.

That night we were relieved.

The Ypres salient saw some of the war's bloodiest battles. In September-October 1917 Australians spearheaded three 'step by step' battles in the salient, each designed to batter down and occupy a limited depth of the German defences guarding Passchendaele. Each Australian battalion, following newly introduced regulations, left behind twenty officers and 108 men to form the nucleus for a new unit in case the rest of the battalion was wiped out. Even so over 35,000 Australians, half the A.I.F. in France, became casualties in the salient.

The 57th Battalion took part in the second 'step by step' battle, at Polygon Wood. Here Downing, now a sergeant, earned the Military Medal, for an action he does not describe in his book. In the words of his citation, when his senior officers became casualties, Downing 'did most valuable work in organising and despatching carrying parties under very heavy shell fire. By his coolness and courage under trying conditions he set a fine example to all men who came under his command'.

IX

BY THE MENIN ROAD
POLYGON WOOD
26th September 1917
The Third Battle of Ypres

THE MILD afternoon sun of dying autumn made a faint shimmer on the crumbled walls of Ypres, three miles to our north.

The road bore on its torn breast men from Poperinghe and Oudendom and Dickebusch, and from over the rearward hills, to their duty. The trudging feet of heavy-eyed battalions going away from the salient — that bulging semi-circle of death — beat lighter, pitifully lighter on the loosened ground, than the proud thunder of the legions that had marched to receive the myriad hammer-strokes of Thor, and to return blow for blow. The roads in that place have borne the arms of Caesar and Charlemagne and Conde, Alva and Marlborough and Wellington, through the gates of Ypres and past its walls of hard and hoary bricks, and the deep moats where bullfrogs croak among the reeds that grow in the black water. But never have these highways carried more glory or more tragedy than now. Splintered corduroys (rows of logs) wind across the foul mud along the road. On either side is a long mound of wagons, rifles, ambulances, equipment. It leads by Polygon Wood. It is the Menin Road.

Observation balloons sway and turn a little, green-bellied, white-backed in the sun — bizarre, pig-like, with blunt snouts, large ears, and a flapping roll of skin beneath — tethered over Chateau Segard, and on either hand in a line to the horizon.

Chateau Segard lies in heaps between its trees. There are little lakes and summer houses, all overgrown with bushes that straggle over the tumbled ground and over-hang the water. Here the battalions came, footsore from three days of long marches over cobblestones.

We bivouacked. The Black (67th) Battalion, the Brown (59th) Battalion, and the White (60th) Battalion of the Red (15th) Brigade of the 5th Division lay from Cafe Belge on the crossroads to Chateau Segard. The Purple (58th) Battalion went in the line next day, with the Green (14th) Brigade. The Yellow (8th) Brigade was the divisional reserve.

Our sister battalions in the 1st Division were coming 'out'. Theirs had been a relatively easy task. The enemy were in the process of moving a large proportion of their artillery when the attack took place. Their success gave us confidence.

On the 24th the men of the battalions detailed for the attack received extra water bottles, rifle grenades, ammunition, bombs, rockets, sandbags, wire cutters and iron rations. There were conferences held by battalion and company commanders, when the plans of attack were discussed. To some came premonitions of death, as frequently happens — forebodings that are invariably justified. They did not speak of it, but their friends could tell. Most were in good heart. Packs were left behind.

At 3.30 p.m. the battalions moved forward, along the roads, past Ypres and Zillebeke. At evening we came to China Wall, whose bleached untidy sandbags had helped to stop the German rushes in 1914 and 1915. That night there were a number killed and wounded while they slept in their dugouts. The front line was about four miles away. Incendiary shells fell by the adjacent dumps in thunderous crashes, then flamed and flared and seemed to die away, and flared again with a ruddy blaze whose reflection was visible for forty miles. The barrage was seven miles deep. Batteries of giant guns were at our elbows, firing ear-splitting salvos on roads and villages far in the enemy's country. Stretcher-bearers passed to and fro upon the duckboards. The front line seemed comparatively quiet. A few flares rose gracefully, like daffodils in the sky.

Next morning there was a fatigue forward. Stokes shells had to be carried to Clapham Junction, where there were four or five concrete blockhouses, a trench, some derelict tanks and the end of an old German tunnel. Bodies lay here and there along the track, stray tragedies of the night and morning. Shelling grew hotter. A few only were hit. At midday the parties returned through Sanctuary Wood to China Wall. We ate heavily without taste or appetite, rested a few minutes and moved forward in groups of six in single file at intervals of eighty yards.

We came to the barren, pitted hills by Hooge Crater as the sun was setting. Below and far away were Ypres and Zillebeke and the Lake, where bursting shells shot geysers of water high in the air. Shells fell here and there, on all the country before and behind. We dug in.

We had a feeling of sinking through space. Men fell silent, or spoke casually, or made surly jests, according to their natures, commented on the trench that had been made, on the shelter placed to keep out the wind, for we had been sweating, and it was chilly in the shade. Artillery flashed and rumbled unceasingly. We winced as we were jerked by the concussion of shells which burst closer by. We smoked and waited in a kind of lethargy. No one spoke of the task before us. Time dragged on.

Sand and dust trickled down the walls after each concussion. Occasionally we stirred to brush the dirt from our necks and to empty our pockets of dust. Dry heavy clods of earth flew on the air. Fragments of ragged iron whirled and buzzed. Night fell. Shells roared and moaned incessantly across the floor of heaven. The sky was starry. There was a pale horned moon. It was cold.

Despair, hope, despondency and resolution fought for the possession of each soul. Despondency and resolution remained as a sediment in our minds. There was a lull in the shelling. The moon was hidden in clouds. From the darkness all around came the tinkle of harness, the oaths of drivers, the clink of picks and shovels as the artillery pulled into place and dug positions. Wheels made no sound in the dry and crumbled earth. 'The end of the war; the end of the war! Some day, of course. Shall I ever see it? ... Back in Dickebusch there is rest. There is the quiet of sleep; and here, the quiet of death

… Shall I ever see it? … I wonder what the wife is doing, thinking … ' It was not quiet for long.

We were to move forward at one in the morning. Cautiously I covered my head with a waterproof sheet to light a cigarette, carefully concealing the flame and glowing end from the sky. A German plane was throbbing overhead.

At ten o'clock came a sudden order to move. The Purple Battalion was being attacked. Shells fell thicker. Above the firing line flares were slowly rising and curving, interlaced like a thicket of bulrushes. I addressed my friends in a low voice as they went by, each man's scabbard, entrenching tool, and wire cutter swinging and clicking against his shovel and his rifle butt. They passed like black shadows. I took my place and moved along by the old German tunnel, subconsciously counting the places where it was blown in.

There were long waits when we sat and sweated on the sides of shellholes, when the leaders of the string of men were retarded by obstacles. A delay of one second was multiplied by the number of men in that long line. The rear stumbled forward, successively running and halting, always striving to keep in touch with the front. Then the foremost stood and waited. It was a rough road. Shelling grew heavier and heavier as we drew closer to the line. The men were too blown to care very much for that.

At length we bore left from the tunnel. We jumped or climbed across trenches. We passed the blockhouses of Clapham Junction, clattered over sheets of iron from a one-time dug-out, and entered Glencorse Wood, mounting the hill. We were guided by white tapes laid on the ground by battalion scouts some hours before.

There was a crash close by, a red flame, flying sparks. Another — and two men were seen in the flash, toppling stiffly sideways, one to the right, one to the left: the one with a forearm partly raised, the other lifted a little from the ground, with legs and arms spread-eagled wide — all seen in an instant — then a second of darkness, then shells, big shells, flashing and crashing all around. We were caught in the barrage.

No time for caring as we stumbled past the reeking bodies as nearly at a run as our exhaustion permitted — heads down as though it were a hurricane of rain, not ripping steel.

By the red and flickering light of the shellbursts men could be seen running and staggering, bent low. They dropped into what had been a trench, into shellholes, enduring, enduring with tautened faces, lying close to the ground, crouching as they burrowed for dear life with their entrenching tools, while the storm of steel wreaked its fury on tortured earth and tortured flesh. There were on all sides the groans and the wailing of mangled men. A sergeant ran around his platoon. He saw by the flashes bodies twisted and doubled and still, and dying men with eyeballs protruding and slightly wavering, blowing bubbles of blood from their lips as they breathed. Then the top of his skull was lifted from his forehead by a bullet, as on a hinge, and his body fell on two crouching men, washing them with his blood and brains. We were in the front line, but did not immediately know it. The din was frightful. A man with a blackened face and a shattered arm ran bleeding towards the rear. An officer was seen in flashlights yelling in a

76

corporal's ear. The answer was unheard. The corporal moved hither and thither, found what men he could, and motioned them forward. We stumbled from shellhole to shellhole by ones and twos with panting breath and shiny faces. One fell writhing. They disappeared in the flickering luminous smoke. The smell of burnt explosive was thick and pungent. Bodies, living and dead, were buried, tossed up, and the torn fragments buried again.

The shelling slackened half-hour by half-hour. At length there fell a silence broken only by spasms of the slow chatter of German machine-guns close at hand and by the higher note of a Lewis gun on the left. What had been the 57th was now no more than a few handfuls of black-faced men wearily digging.

The 58th Battalion had been heavily attacked. Though it had driven back the enemy from its own front, Highland Light Infantry, Argyle and Sutherland Highlanders and the Middlesex, on right and left, suffering terribly against heavy odds, had fallen back. The Australians then found themselves attacked on three sides, bombed and fired on from both flanks and from even their rear. They steadily drove off successive hordes of Germans from their front, a task which alone might have severely tested many times their number. Shattered by a barrage, weakened still further by bloody fighting, this gallant battalion held on under shelling, under merciless fire from its flanks, and under impact after impact on the men that nevertheless stood always like a wall, bayoneting the Huns that penetrated their screen of bullets.

What they did next is worthy of remembrance.

From the weak battalion weak parties were detached to counter-attack right and left, to bomb along the trench and to re-establish almost an entire brigade front, while the remainder held the enemy at arm's length. Each venture had less than a gambler's chance, each was a desperately forlorn hope. They succeeded, and God and many an unknown hero, who fell with a ring of German dead about him, alone know how.

Meanwhile the 57th Battalion had been pushed forward to fill the one remaining gap. It was the fate of a British army that was disputed upon that mile of line.

There was intense activity in the various headquarters. When at length it was seen that the situation had cleared, it was decided to carry out the original plan of attack. Neither the 57th nor the 58th Battalion could now be used as a striking force. The 29th and the 31st were therefore sent forward in their place. The 59th and 60th were to attack with them. The shattered remainder of the 57th and 58th provided stretcher-bearers, ammunition carriers, 'mopping up' parties (to clear the conquered ground of nests of lurking Germans) and supports and reinforcements for the leading waves.

In Glencorse Wood the night wore on. Enemy aircraft buzzed overhead. Machine-guns and snipers swept the ground. We squeezed our bodies into the bottom of our narrow potholes, and drowsed and shivered.

At the oncoming of dawn the sky behind flamed like the Aurora Borealis. Immediately there was a mighty rushing sound as cohorts of shells streamed in thousands over the light mist. In that instant came a roar as of the dissolution of the universe — the guns. Multitudinous sharp and clattering thunders mingled in one deafening and tumultuous banging like the beating of a million tin cans. Six thousand guns, wheel by wheel, firing thirty thousand shells a minute, flung a thunderous ribbon on the German lines, weaving to and fro like the shuttle on a loom, combing the country with intersecting teeth that passed and repassed.

At the same time there was a tapping and a chattering as hundreds of machine-guns, sounding in the infrequent lulling of the barrage like a leit motif in Wagnerian music, sprayed lead behind the German lines — 'a shell per minute, a bullet per second to every ten square yards of ground'.

It had been impossible to conceal the imminence of this battle, and the enemy was well prepared. Our artillery radiated outwards. Theirs fired inwards from the circumference of the salient and was therefore concentrated on any focus which commended itself to German artillerists. Ours could fire frontally only. Theirs enfiladed any of our trenches from three sides. The strength of the hostile barrage was about equal to ours.

Yesterday Glencorse had been a wood on a ridge, now it was only a mound of splintered stumps amid the dust. Looking forward one saw the irregular line of blockhouses captured by the 1st Division six days before. Those were one hundred yards away. On the edge of Polygon Wood, about eight hundred yards further ahead, was a maze of trenches called Black Watch Corner, and a very strong pillbox named Cameron House. Beyond was the Racecourse in a fold in the ground. On the horizon was a high, short ridge, jagged like a dog's teeth, sometimes called the Butte of Polygon.

Shells were drawn to Glencorse as the sparks fly upward. Men habitually shelter in woods from rain or death, and the enemy artillery was probably trained on it days before. It was a high place and a landmark, the presumable location of a trench. Through it all supplies, ammunition and reinforcements for the front line had to pass. In any case, the enemy always put a barrage just behind our front line. There the risk to his own troops of variation in ranging was small.

The dust of that threshing floor obscured the sun. The shelling of the previous night was a circumstance to this. Within five minutes the place was covered by shell-holes overlapped on many sides by others. There were flesh and blood in this hell. A dozen stretcher-bearers and wounded men were killed in the doorway of the regimental aid post as they were entering it in a group. The barrage continued without intermission for twenty-four hours, and what the men endured could never be described, for the effect of shell fire is horrifying out of all proportion to the number it mangles and kills. Each inch of ground was tossed and churned and churned a thousand times. The little trenches were obliterated in the first five minutes. Scores of the survivors of the night were buried alive or blown to fragments.

Mostly, the blockhouses stood. Concrete four feet thick and reinforced with many layers of half-inch steel rods will stand anything. Yet even these forts were cracked and battered. The entrances of their single doors were jammed with the bodies of dead and dying men who had taken refuge there. The interiors were filled with officers who bore heavy responsibilities, hard at work. The floors were foul with blood and brains and viscera and dirt, trampled in by panting runners. The air was noxious with the fumes of burnt T.N.T. A kind of white sand from the explosive settled after each burst. Hour after hour this continued. There was never a sign of slackening.

The attack was rapidly pressed to its objective. The smashed divisions of the Hun recoiled. They were probably in a like purgatory.

The 29th, 31st and 59th were the first wave or rather, series of waves. Next came the 60th and numbers of the 57th and 58th, now dealing with enemy machine-gun posts which had lain low till the leading waves had passed over, now assisting the steel edge of the attack, now capturing Cameron House and other strong places that were holding back the labouring troops of the United Kingdom on the flank; till at length the whole line flung forward to the final objective, fifteen hundred yards from the 'lie-out' position.

While the new line was being dug the 57th and 58th carried forward ammunition and supplies, returning with wounded — exhausting work, and no less hazardous than the actual fighting. Prisoners were straggling back in large parties escorted by single men. A few Fokkers that had penetrated our screen of aeroplanes, which was set far forward in the sky, were bombing and gunning our men. They withdrew on the approach of some Australian airmen who flew low and waved to the infantry. The German barrage increased its extent to the newly won ground, without slackening its fury. There was an air fight so high that the little gleaming specks were barely visible. One fell in flames, with a trail of black smoke that reached to earth.

The interminable shattering horror continued as the first day became the second night, and the second night wore into the second day.

When effort was vital a madness enlivened limbs heavy with fatigue. The numbness of exhaustion kept a guard on reason, dulling a little the full realisation of this agony; and ever the mangling, ripping thunderbolts crashed rapidly as a roll of kettle drums.

Men dragged their buried bodies from under the tossing waves of earth. That most awful sound, the muffled voice of a man buried under three feet of dirt, was heard not seldom, like a ventriloquist, far away — 'Dig me out, dig me out!' They were almost invariably dead by the time they were disinterred.

Men lay in lethargy, eyes sunken, faces drawn and old and smeared with blood. Their voices were ghostly whispers, their throats crusty and dry. Thirst added a fresh misery.

In the morning of the second day the barrage slackened, then ceased. We discovered with wonder that we were hungry. There were holes through water bottles, haversacks were rent and full of dirt. One sought food and water among the dead, muttering, 'Pardon, brother, you don't need it.'

At ten, the barrage began again. At about five in the afternoon the storm became a hurricane, and the S.O.S., a triple rocket of portent, red over green over yellow, rose from the front line.

All the men who could be scraped together were sent forward. Runners came panting and stumbling into the different battalion headquarters near Glencorse, with messages appealing for more water, more ammunition. There was now scarcely anyone to carry it, but occasional parties were returning with supplies from a little further back, which had previously been placed in dumps. Two signallers with a telephone line on a reel between them came running from the front, the reel unwinding behind them and laying the line. Five minutes later they were forward again, mending it in a score of places. Parties of almost utterly exhausted men were sent up. Among others a group of thirty men stumbled forward, carrying the heavy bomb and ammunition boxes, and petrol tins full of water, unable to move faster than a crawl, but striving willingly for the sake of the line and their comrades. The party was reduced to sixteen in the first thousand yards. The N.C.O. in charge placed eight in one portion of an old trench, seven in another, for they could go no further without rest, and himself went ahead to reconnoitre the ground. On returning to the eight he found them stripped, chopped into lumps like butcher's meat, mixed, indistinguishable, all dead. He shambled, wild-eyed, to the seven. They were likewise. He threw his steel helmet far away and sat down. His body seemed shrunken. 'This is the finish, the finish,' he whispered from cracked and blackened lips. These things had been happening for forty-eight hours. He lifted a damaged water tin and drank deep. Then he took two full tins and struggled up and down the steep sliding sides of shellholes till at length he fell into the front line. He raised himself, picked up a German rifle, and quietly began firing at the enemy who were swarming like bull ants from shellhole to shellhole.

At length the counter-attack was repulsed. Quiet

and night came slowly.

The 59th and 60th were by now reduced to much the same proportions as the remainder of the brigade. The men began sullenly digging deeper and deeper. Word came that the relief was expected at ten that night.

The minutes passed like centuries. At ten past ten the relief arrived, after the garrison had almost given up hope. Platoon and company commanders hurriedly gathered their men, who needed no second telling, and proceeded as fast as they were able to Chateau Segard. Life holds no pleasure comparable with the joy of being relieved. We were a pathetic band, with dirty faces and stubbly beards. All were hysterical in varying degrees.

We walked, the strong supporting the weak, through Polygon and Glencorse Woods, now one with the barren desolation behind, past Clapham Junction, Zouave Wood, and by Hooge to Hellfire Corner and Halfway House. Here we were given coffee. We limped into the huts behind the trees of Chateau Segard towards dawn of the third day of the attack, the fourth of the battle, the fifth under the barrage. We ate and drank, then slept like the dead.

The flames in the sky, the rumble of the guns continued, but we heeded nothing.

X

JACK O'LANTERN ON BROODSEINDE

Bluey AND I were sitting under a water-proof sheet in our dugout one night in the support line on the near side of Broodseinde ridge, smoking as we listened to the 'gezumphs' bursting on the Line. Bluey is a person of parts. We should have been on a fatigue, burying a telephone cable on the top of a ridge, but Bluey had casually mentioned to the O.C. (Officer Commanding) that he knew where to find some galvanised iron that wouldn't be bad for making dugouts. The O.C. would never associate himself with anything so immoral as 'snavelling'; but neither of us was detailed for the fatigue.

Well, we were sitting in our dugout, when who should blow in but Nugget Evans! He had been told we were here. He was a second corporal in the engineers. Yes, he was on the cable party, supervising dopey infantry. We pushed him against the wall of the dugout, both together, with our feet, and held him there. He kamaraded.

Bluey produced a water bottle, but it didn't contain water. I should have told you that Bluey was no dope.

After a time, I was just going to mention that the King of North Carolina was about to send another note to the Queen of South Carolina, when Bluey pushed a tin hat over my face. Bluey never does anything without a reason, so I looked towards the trench. Right in the doorway was a pair of fat legs encased in trench boots and riding breeches. It was old Bully Beef. I'd know those legs in a thousand. I've seen them kicking when his horse cantered, too many times not to.

'Where are those runners? Dear me —.'

Someone came skooshing in the mud, from the runners' dugout. We heard an anxious whispering.

'Go at once to battalion headquarters and tell the C.O. that there are some men in the reserve line who ought to be on the cable fatigue. Er — no; perhaps I'd better go. You come and guide me.'

Bluey whispered to me and he whispered to Nugget. I was a bit doubtful and Nug was a bit stung, but Bluey isn't one to be disregarded under any circumstances.

We blew out the candle and crawled into the trench. Bully walked away, the runner following. I quietly put my arm over the runner's mouth and yanked him into the dugout. He was nasty at first, but I had a peacemaker with me. He saw reason straight away, so I put back the cork and let him go. Meanwhile Nugget had gone off with Bully in the runner's place.

Next day we came out to Ouderdom. The colonel had all the runners before him while Bull questioned them. 'No,' said he, 'it wasn't any of them — and yet I'm sure I'd know his voice.'

I didn't see Nugget till one night two months later at the engineers' dump by Irish House, on the Wytschaete front. He laughed when he saw me. I asked him what he did with old Bully Beef that night. He told me. I walked along the duckboards, letting the full glory of it sink in. Then I sat on the edge of a shell hole and laughed till I couldn't get up.

He took old Bully by a 'short cut' across country — all the country. He pulled him out of every shellhole in the sector, and led him into every old trench. Being half blotto, he switched on his electric torch — a mad thing to do, for the night was pitchy dark, and it could be seen for miles. Poor fat old Bully Beef followed that light over miles of country, ignorant of his whereabouts, gasping with consternation and shortness of wind; demanding, begging the 'guide' to say if he knew the way, getting no response, ordering, imploring him to put out the light — 'over bog, over fen', till Nugget flashed the dazzling light in his eyes and a gun flash revealed — the Cloth Hall of Ypres! He turned to his 'guide' (I spluttered to think of the word) and found himself alone. His will-of-the-wisp had disappeared.

I think I said Bluey was a person of parts.

XI

HOLDING THE LINE
(MESSINES RIDGE)
November and December 1917
January to March 1918

WINTER BEGAN while the Australians were at
Passchendaele and Broodseinde. Conditions were similar to Flers, but though the valleys were flooded, the
mud in the trenches on the high ground was rarely
deeper than the knees. The shelling, however, was far
heavier than on the Somme. Otherwise all that has been
said about the previous winter applied to this. The mud
was awful. The Australian Corps was moved at the
beginning of November to the sector comprising the
hills on the right of Ypres, and the villages of
Wytschaete, Messines, Warneton, and Ploegsteert. At
first the trenches were waterlogged. In some parts of the
line there were duckboards. Duckwalks led to the front
trenches. The various headquarters were installed in
concrete blockhouses which had been either captured in
June or built by our engineers. Pumps were used to cope

with the flooding of the trenches. Patrols in no man's land were frequently bogged for hours.

The rains came, the frosty nights bound our world in ice, it snowed. Snowstorms were the characteristic feature of this winter. They drifted unrelentingly down. The great flakes found their way through the smallest chinks in our shelters and filled our dugouts with fluffy heaps that melted and soaked us. Outside, the white drifts were feet deep. The snow showed black paths beaten in the previous night. The thaw filled our shallow trenches to the brim with chilly slush.

The enterprise of our troops and the increasing activity of the enemy made what had been a quiet sector a place where there were little actions nightly. The line grew rougher and rougher. There were patrol fights, and raids both by us and by the enemy; sometimes there were two raids in a night on the one company front. Shelling was continual and heavy. Minenwerfer barrages made day hideous and night a long agony. Tours of duty were unusually long — six or seven days in the front line, then the same length of time in close supports. It was as hot and trying a time as ever we had. The German line was crammed with minenwerfers. Ours was crammed with men.

We had news of scores of divisions from Russia that were accumulated in camps behind the German lines. Hence there were many raids to locate and identify German units. We awaited the onslaught with confidence, though not with equanimity. We feverishly dug trenches, built strong points in carefully selected sites, and refortified the pill-boxes.

We knew our power in defence, but realised that all

men are equal before an obliterating barrage such as we were aware might be flung on us at any time. We knew that when it came not many of the garrison would survive, but we were determined that those who escaped it would give a good account of themselves.

We expected it every morning and every evening. We stood to arms and waited. December passed, and it did not come. January went out in frost, and February in snowstorms; March came and still there was no offensive.

Prisoners gave varying dates for the commencement of their onslaught. 'The beginning of spring' was as specific as they knew. One morning, immediately after the hour of stand down, we were awakened by music in the German lines. Bugles were blowing far and near. Green flares were rising in the air, although it was no longer night. We hurriedly manned our posts. We had never heard anything like this before. But nothing happened. By day we dared not move even within our trenches lest the enemy should locate us.

From a cylindrical concrete heap thirty feet high — the Warneton Tower — the Germans could look into our trenches. Light shells had no effect on it. The big 9.2 howitzers merely chipped flakes of concrete away and bared a few steel rods. At length a great eleven-inch cannon on railway mountings was brought to the sector. Its heavy boom started the birds in the trees by Wervicq and Comines, three miles across the valley in enemy country. The first shell burst with a mighty roar. It missed. So did the second, third, and fourth. The fifth shell fell at the base of the solid structure. There was a cloud of dust. As it cleared we saw the mass heel over, oblique to the ground. The earth shuddered as it fell. Dozens of Germans must have been killed within it.

At length we went back to Wulverghem. While we were there we went to the line each night as wiring parties or to dig strong points. The minenwerfers gave no respite by night or day. There were thirteen firing on the company sector, on a front of four hundred yards! Their dreadful missiles searched the ground till they found our posts. Some of the latter received continual attention, and we were unable to use them. The minenwerfers had a range of fourteen hundred yards. We strained our ears for their distant pop. Sometimes quick eyes saw them, like short pencil-stubs, turning over and over, poising, then falling like arrows as we watched the sky. We scarcely dared look at the ground. They always seemed to be falling directly on one. The guns fired from deep round pits. The minenwerfer shells were about four feet long, and their craters were big enough to put a house in. We saw them falling on us and were rooted to the spot with horror, for we never knew which way to run. They swerved about fifty feet from the ground, by reason of some mechanical attachment. A few fell straight. One lived centuries as they fell.

There would be a faint pop in the German lines. Everyone looked tensely upwards. 'Look out!' Down we dropped, grinding our teeth as we waited for a long, long second. BOOM! The trench rocked like a ship at sea. Lumps of earth from the size of a cricket ball to a piano hurtled over us. BOOM! BOOM! Unconsciously a man was gripping the ankle of an unnoticing mate. The latter was lamed for days. Still they fell, and the ground quivered and swayed and pitched. This barrage lasted for hours. At nightfall we visited the next post. A minenwerfer had fallen in it. Every man was dead.

One night the enemy attempted to raid, and was beaten back. Next morning a German approached under the white flag to ask permission to recover the wounded. It was granted. The Huns found means to observe the position of one of our posts. That night it was blown out.

★

The four of us were waiting in the trench while the sergeant was receiving his instructions in the company headquarters dugout. He reappeared. 'Right-oh. All got bags tied round your bayonets? All got bombs?' He led the way to one of our outposts. We sat and waited while a runner went around all the posts and warned their garrisons that we were going out on patrol and informed them when and where we would return. The sergeant disappeared into the dugout of the officer in charge of the post. After a time he called us in. There was a bottle of whisky and a little metal cup. The officer poured out a stiff dose for each. 'Happy days, Mr. Evans.' He grinned at us. Boom! The concussion put out the candle. Minenwerfers! We crawled into the trench. The night was black as the pit. When no flares were going up we could see absolutely nothing, except a skyline which was slightly blacker than the heavens. We went along our barbed wire, half feeling our way, half chancing to luck in the darkness. Shells were bursting every few minutes. Five minenwerfers soared up and up, spreading parallel trails of fire overhead, and thundered together far behind us. A Stokes gun was coughing on the left. Its shells were crashing in a noisy heap.

In the line, never a sound is heard that does not mean death.

The sergeant led the way through a gap in the wire. We worked from shell-hole to shell-hole, until we were fifty yards out, knowing well that we could vaguely be seen against the skyline. We lay for half an hour without moving a muscle, straining our eyes for a sight of the enemy, listening for the sounds of movement. Then, cautiously, we moved further forward. For an hour we lay motionless. We heard voices in the German line, fifty yards away. The five of us were in diamond formation, a man at each corner and one in the centre. The sergeant went first. We stopped when he stopped, moved whenever he moved. At length he crawled back and told us to stay where we were while he went forward to examine the enemy wire. He crept away. We spread out and faced to right and left, ready to keep at bay any German who might come before he could return. A minenwerfer was firing within sixty yards of us. It was its crew whom we had heard talking. After a long wait the sergeant came back. He whispered to Snowy, 'Go back to Lieutenant Brown as fast as you can, and report that the Hochs have cut their own wire opposite Number Eleven Post. You can tell him we've located that new minenwerfer. You needn't come back.' The matter was serious. It meant an enemy 'stunt' — a raid, at the least.

With infinite caution we worked along the German wire, one man at a time. We found a body sprawled across some strands of wire. When would we be like that

— so shrivelled, so grey? Sooner or later, for it appears there is no way out, except by losing a limb. Rats ran away squeaking. Bang! A flare fizzled upwards. We lay flat. We saw the dead man's face. It was a poor beggar reported missing after the raid a week ago. One arm hung down, the hand lightly touching the ground. All the fingers were gone, gnawed off. Bot cut the string of his identity disc and took it. We moved on.

Suddenly the sergeant stopped and clicked his tongue. We all dropped into shellholes. Figures of men loomed through the darkness. By the faint light of a distant flare we saw them. One — two — five — eight — eleven — fourteen. They wore helmets like coal-scuttles. We lay still, our nerves on edge. One repressed a mad desire to yell. They passed within inches of us, several times brushing our faces with their boots. One of them stood on Graham's hand. Fortunately the ground was very soft. Fortunately also, no flare went up, though naturally the Huns were not firing them while their own patrol was out. For once we blessed the pitchy darkness. It seemed years before they passed along, but at length they went. We rose. It was a bad fright. Our hands were shaking. We crawled away.

There was a muffled curse from the sergeant. We went to him. We were among more wire. We had to stand upright to climb over. Luckily it was a great deal blown about by shelling. At length Graham whispered that he was through. As we were about to join him we heard the Hun patrol coming back — in front of the wire. Then we understood how nearly we had walked into the German trench. There was no time to drop. The wire would have made too much noise. We took bombs from our pockets, and loosened the springs. Holding down the detonating-spring-levers in our grasp, so that they would explode only when we threw them, we drew out the pins with our teeth. We waited, a bomb in either hand. We thought we saw the sergeant raise his arm. We watched for him to throw. A wire sprang back and clanged against an iron screw. The Germans heard it. In a faint, brief flicker of some distant light, we saw them hesitate. As the sergeant threw his bombs, we threw ours. There were six crashes, six flames. There were groans and wails and shouts and a medley of voices. Under cover of the confusion we sprang over the last of the wire and ran for our lives, scattering. The Germans were firing their rifles. Judging by the position of the flashes they also were retiring. We moved away, keeping low in the cover of shellholes.

Then the enemy machine-guns opened fire. The Huns must have run back to their trench. For twenty minutes bullets whizzed over us. When it grew quiet, we rejoined the sergeant.

'Where's Bot?' said he. We tried to pierce the gloom.

'He may have gone in.'

'He may have been knocked. We'll have to go back.'

We retraced the tedious way, carefully as before. We found four dead Germans and one wounded one, but no Bot. We cautiously searched the ground without result. We gathered together again. We conferred in whispers.

'He must have gone back alone — or else he's captured. Come on.'

'We'll take this souvenir with us, though.' A flare

shot up. We lay still until it burned out. The German, apparently unconscious, was breathing stentoriously. We dragged him as we crawled, then, when at a comparatively safe distance, picked him up and carried him. We walked for a little way, bending low. Flares were rising at intervals, apparently from all directions. The sergeant stopped and looked about him.

'We've lost our way, I think.'

It was certainly very baffling. The German line curved backwards in a horse shoe, and we had to find the narrow opening, so as to avoid running into German wire. One experience of that was quite enough for the night. There were absolutely no landmarks, the stars were obscured by clouds, and we had no compass. Another flare rose and revealed us standing. A rifle bolt rattled. We could not have endured much more.

'Halt!'

One of our listening posts!

We gave the password, 'Essendon'. The sentry directed us to the nearest outpost. We entered the dugout. Bot was sitting inside, having a wound dressed. A fragment of his own bomb had hit him in the shoulder.

The prisoner began to mutter and wriggle.

'Only stunned, I think.'

We made our way through minenwerfers to company headquarters. Boxes were standing in a pile. The rations had come. The sergeant went into a dugout to write his report, and to trace our course on a patrol map.

'Kept any tucker for us?'

'In those hot-boxes. Stew and tea. When you're ready you can get a drink of rum from Corporal McKay.

There's an issue of cigarettes tonight.'

'Good-oh.'

*

The afternoon was quiet. During the previous night our patrols had reported that two large German blockhouses, The Elephant and The Giant, in front of our trench, were strongly occupied, and that trenches had been dug about them. At seven o'clock the enemy began to shell. At nine he concentrated minenwerfers on our post. Luckily most of them fell behind us. It was none the less very terrible. We were ordered to go forward to the shellholes among our wire. A minenwerfer fell in the trench. We went farther forward. Two men were sent out to act as a listening post. Suddenly the barrage ceased. The men came running back.

'The Fritzes are coming over. Hundreds of them.'

'Back to the trench then!'

We ran to it. Only the ends were left. In the centre was a yawning crater. On the enemy came, a long line of indistinct figures, shoulder to shoulder. We poured rapid fire into them. Many dropped. The rest kept resolutely on. Our fire was knocking them over in scores. Our two Lewis guns were sweeping the ground. We fired till the heated woodwork of our rifles burnt our hands, saying to ourselves, 'They mustn't reach the trench. There'll be hell to pay if they do. We must keep 'em off, we must, we must.' The machine-gunners were cursing the Germans at the top of their voices as they rattled pan after pan of bullets into them. Several of our men lay at the bottom of the trench, very quiet. Others were groaning.

The outpost was about forty yards long. There was bombing on the left. A party of Germans had got through our wire farther up, and were coming in behind. They bombed our men from that end of the trench back to the crater in the middle. The Huns in front had stopped and were firing from shellholes. They now ceased fire. Our men on the right were keeping their heads down. The wire in front of them was very strong.

We gathered all the bombs we could, and rushed to the left along the top of a trench, flinging them ahead of us. The Germans retreated before us. Then we attempted to charge with the bayonet, but were driven back by showers of bombs, leaving several dead. There were now not many of us left. We were reinforced by a party from the post on the right of ours.

Once more we almost drove the enemy off. We fought as far as our supply of bombs would take us, then the Huns pushed us back until their bombs ran out. Twice they drove us to the extreme right end, and twice we forced them back. The last time the enemy turned tail and surged back through a gap in the wire. They had seen strong reinforcements coming from the post on the left, and another party from our rear.

Hot work!

Following the Russian Revolution in November 1917 there was peace between Germany and Russia. A large number of German troops were moved from the east to the Western Front and a major offensive began on 21 March.

XII

STEMMING THE RUSH
27th March to 15th April 1917

'THE ENEMY will shortly attack us. You will find yourselves heavily outnumbered. Your experiences of Bullecourt and Polygon Wood will be mere circumstances compared with what you will be forced to endure. It will be your duty to fight to the last, if attacked; and we know you will do it.'

So were we told.

The Australian divisions waited on the vital ridge of Messines. Night and day the men dug defences, toiling like galley slaves, but nothing happened. The 1st Division was relieved, and after a brief spell returned to the line; the Third and Fourth moved to their rest area, and still we strained our eyes in the faint lights of dusk and dawn, tensely awaiting the hurricane that did not come.

And then the blow fell, but not at Messines. There were wild and contradictory reports of terrible disaster to our arms, of bloody repulses of the enemy. Rumours ran fast from lip to lip. On a morning the impedimenta of battle were issued; we were suddenly ordered to parade in marching order, and to abandon every surplus article.

We marched to Bailleul. Heavy shells were falling in the old town. There was a fevered bustle at the siding where we clambered into the long trains which, as they drew from the station, were pursued by bursting shells. One train was hit.

All night long we shivered in the darkness of the crowded cattle-truck. All night long the carriages rattled and bumped as we smoked and wondered towards what dreadful things we were being taken. To our disordered fancies — for we had already been for two continuous months in the line — the vision of Death seemed to be riding the engine. So we drowsed and were wakened by the jolting of the truck, or by the discomfort of the hard corners of the heaps of rifles and equipment on which we were huddled, forty men in a space of fifteen feet by nine; and our dreams were of heavy things.

The cold light of morning brought the chimneys and the brick houses of Doullens. The train stopped with a jerk. A bugle blew a note, and we stretched our cramped limbs and scrambled stiffly from the train, dragging our heavy equipment. We began a march of which we knew not the goal, of which we knew only that it would be long and weary.

At first, movement was pleasant, for it brought warmth to our chilled bodies. Then we came to desire more and more strongly the brief respite at the end of every hour, until our pack straps cut into our shoulders, and our water bottles chafed our hips, and our feet grew bruised and blistered on the cobbles that alternated with muddy roads and broken metal. We marched through a long, long morning, through a weary afternoon, through half the night, being continually urged to greater efforts. We spoke thickly like drunken men, for we were burdened with sleep. We staggered as we stepped into our fours for each successive stretch of marching, and then strode forward with a precision that was only mechanical. The weight of our gear was a torture.

And when at last we came to the barns and outhouses of the ramshackle village where we were to sleep that night, and had eaten, we fell sound asleep, too tired to unroll our blankets.

Long before daylight we were aroused by someone stumbling among the pigsties, shouting in a thick voice, 'Reveille, reveille!' We rose stiffly, shivering in the cold night air. We took a hurried breakfast, and marched away.

Our bruised feet pounded on the stones, but their pain was numbed after the first few miles. We climbed the crest of a hill where the road rose high, and far on our right was Amiens Cathedral, touched with fire in the glory of the morning, outlined against a pale green sky. Here was surely something to fight for, a symbol of France, the strong pillar of our Alliance. Over a hillside close at hand a squadron of French cavalry came trotting in a long line, two abreast, in sky-blue cloaks and blue enamelled helmets.

We plodded on all day, tramping past the kilometre stones until we lost their tally, forcing the pace for miles and miles and more interminable miles. There were short halts for meals, when the men flung themselves down, too weary to remove their packs. We went through towns and villages, over cobblestones, cart tracks and high roads. Night found us still shambling along, keeping the step, but with stumbling feet and hanging heads. The desire for sleep was a dull pain; rest seemed the sweetest thing in the world, but we bit our tongues and kept going. We drowsed as we marched, literally walking in our sleep, and in the five-minute halts at the end of every hour we dropped to the ground and slept. Some mechanically kept walking; we called to them to make them stop.

At length, after I know not how many miles, by the faint moonlight we saw the two towers of Corbie church, and the shining patches of the Somme lagoons in a valley.

We straggled into the town. That night we slept in houses. The inhabitants had fled, leaving the bread in the oven, the fire in the stove, the soup in the pot. The place was mutely pitiful; there were toys of children, the little intimate things of families, cottages wrecked by the shells which were already bursting. We found good wine, and slept well.

The 3rd Division had driven forward from Corbie and had met retiring English, who told them that 'Jerry was coming over the next hill!' The enemy scouts, however, were not encountered until the Australians had gone several miles. That was in the pelting rain of March the twenty-seventh. At the same time, the 4th Division, moving ahead from Warloy and Contay, had struck the Huns at Buire and Dernancourt, where we had so often been billeted in 1916 and 1917.

The 5th and 2nd Divisions arrived hot-foot from the

North. The 1st Division, following after, were turned back to meet another flood of Germans pouring through the gap they had burst in the British line between Festubert and La Basséle.

On the Somme our line was very thin, and there were great spaces defended only by the machine-guns of aeroplanes in the sky. The first few days were tided over by the efforts of the New Zealanders, the Australians, the British cavalry (fighting on foot); by General Carey's 'scratch division' of labour companies, railwaymen, slightly wounded from the field ambulances, and even a few Americans; and by the heroic deeds of many a worn and shattered British unit, which had already borne the brunt of the first terrible week, after which nothing but a miracle could have saved the Allies from total defeat. That miracle was, under God, provided by the A.I.F.

A provisional front was established. No man's land was wide and indefinite. At first there were affairs of outposts, patrol fights in villages, skirmishes over the hills. Bedridden civilians were rescued from Buire and Hamelet and Verre-sur-Corbie.

On 4th April the 9th Brigade, on the Australian right flank, repulsed with their rifles an attack in apparently overwhelming force at a town destined later to be a shrine to Australian arms — Villers-Bretonneux.

On April the fifth a most determined attempt was made to smash the extreme left of our corps position, at Dernancourt, about fifteen miles to the north-east of the battlefield of the previous day. The Huns came on in masses, field guns among the leading waves. The stand of the 12th and 13th Brigades ranks among the most heroic feats of the war. They slaughtered their enemies in swathes with rifle and machine-gun, but the grey waves kept coming on, too many for our men to kill a tenth. Almost submerged beneath an ocean of foes, surrounded, their flanks beaten in, the Australians fought back to back for hours with bullet and bayonet and bomb; until their supports cut a passage through the German masses, and helped the front line garrison to hurl the enemy back.

Of their number, a bare third were still standing, mostly wounded. The sunken road they had held was a veritable shambles, but the ground about it was literally hidden with German dead. The enemy brought field guns to the hedges and sunken roads within five hundred yards of our position, and almost smothered the thin line of khaki with shells.

There were now very few left. One might think that their spirit would have been battered out of them by that time. They had already won an imperishable glory. But they rose, 'bloody but unbowed', and actually charged the German hordes. That handful of survivors drove the enemy back for half a mile, advancing in the face of attacking stormtroops.

Meanwhile, the whole Australian line, and the New Zealanders on the left, and the British and the French were fighting hard. An Englishman was conferring with one of our generals, and is reported to have said, 'I am putting my men in here. Will yours hold ?' 'WHAT?' shouted the Australian.

They held. The A.I.F. had never lost a trench, nor did they here. That night the line was consolidated under heavy shelling. Stragglers of several nationalities were absorbed by the battalions. Bridge-head positions were thrown across the Somme near Vaire and Hamelet. The weakness of our artillery was a cause of anxiety, for all the guns had not yet arrived from the north. The enemy, moreover, apart from their normal strength in guns, were in possession of all the Russian artillery and many guns lost in the retreat of our Fifth Army. Against that, at least one division possessed, for a time, only four guns; and bluffed the enemy by placing tree trunks in gun pits, and by galloping from place to place by night, firing a shell here and a salvo elsewhere. It is hardly to be wondered that the German staffs claimed to have located thirteen Australian divisions, and to have exterminated five.

We marched in fighting order from Corbie, the rain in our faces. It was the night after our arrival in the old town. We followed sunken roads, crossed fields, slipped and floundered as we climbed muddy banks. We reached a place where shells were bursting frequently, and dug trenches about four feet deep. We were hungry and sodden and muddy and miserable before we had done. The German artillery was flashing before us, but our own was silent, except for a few shots at rare intervals. Our machine-guns opened fire as soon as we reached that place, and strong patrols went forward. This had been done to impress the enemy. But we had no sooner completed our potholes than the patrols returned, and we were ordered to get our gear together. We filed along the front, across more fields, over more sunken roads, over land torn by shells, where the going was heavy. We halted on a hill top, and after several hours' hard work, dug ourselves in. Machine-guns were fired, and patrols were sent out again. Then away we went once more, stumbling, heavy-limbed, heavy-eyed, from place to place all night, without food, and unutterably weary.

At dawn we were on the famous Hill 104. All day we sat in our potholes, soaked to the skin, foul with mud, unable to rest, for a heavy and continuous barrage played upon us from five in the morning till ten at night, smashing one post after another, killing and mangling the occupants. All night long we marched from point to point, now digging, now fighting for our lives with enemy patrols, now simply getting shelled. Next day we were bombarded again. On the third night we marched and dug and fought, fought and dug and marched, faint with hunger, light-headed for want of sleep. The enemy shelled and shelled. At evening a little cold stew and tepid cocoa reached us. We ate like wolves, for it was three days since some of us had eaten, four since we had slept. One prayed for a wound so that one might rest and be warm.

At about nine, in the morning of the sixth of April, after further hours of shelling, we received orders to attack. Such was our exhaustion that we could hardly carry our rifles. In artillery formation, we advanced to the summit of Hill 104, extended into single lines, and as we walked down the forward slopes, we were met with a hail of bullets from a wood seven hundred yards in front. A number of men were hit, so we fell flat, then by twos and threes crawled forward. At length we succeeded in digging a line under heavy machine-gun fire, while shrapnel crashed above our heads. The shelling grew more and more hellish all day, but the Germans who had commenced to trickle through a wide gap in the line retired to their wood, and for the time being any further German advance was impossible.

That night we held the line, so weary that we could scarcely stand, unable to keep our eyes open for five minutes on end. It was only by a terrific effort of will that we kept awake until midnight, and we were withdrawn to a support position a little way behind, and somebody else took over the firing line.

During the succeeding days the enemy's pressure slackened little by little. The harassing forays and little raids by our men showed him that our morale was high. He had already been persuaded by the fierceness of the resistance that our line was strongly held, far more strongly than was actually the case. At length the high commands were able to announce that the character of the fighting was no longer that of a rearguard action.

One incident is worth recording. The 58th Battalion, finding itself too far advanced, sent orders to some of its outposts to retire about a thousand yards. A corporal and four men in a post near Vaire Wood refused to go back. Towards them advanced a party of Germans, led by an officer and a warrant officer. The corporal, after sending back a man to tell what he was about to do, went out from the post with his three men, in broad daylight, without support or the possibility of assistance, and attacked the Germans. After a burst of rapid fire, in which the warrant officer was killed, the four charged the forty. The corporal singled out and killed the officer just as the latter was about to shoot him with his revolver. The Huns wavered and fled, leaving thirteen dead, several wounded, and a number of prisoners.

For the time being Amiens was saved. The inhabitants returned to many of their villages. The sentries, standing ready to explode the mines under every bridge and railway culvert almost to Abbeville, were at length taken away and the mines dismantled.

On 24 April 1918 the Germans captured Villers-Bretonneux on the Somme. In a brilliant counter-attack on Anzac Day, the 5th Division recaptured the village, effectively ending the great German offensive. To this day classrooms in the village school display the sign n'oublions jamais l'Australie—*never forget Australia.*

XIII

THE MIRACLE OF VILLERS-BRETONNEUX
25th April, 1918

ENGLISH BOYS of eighteen and nineteen with a very small leaven of older men took over the heavy responsibility of the sector. They were new to the line — drafts hurried over from England in a time of desperate need. The 8th and 14th Brigades occupied the trenches on their left, the former near Vaire Wood, the latter between them and the English. The 15th were immediately behind both, at Fouilloy and Hamelet and in the Aubigny line, from where they could give prompt aid to the front by Vaire, or Hamel, where the line curved back.

Next morning we stood to arms while French colonials attacked at Hangard Wood and Hangard-en-Santerre, a mile or two on the right of Bretonneux. Here there was heavy fighting, backwards and forwards, day by day. Then for several mornings we stood to arms in the expectation of an attack on the divisional front. It was known that a heavy onset was pending, so we waited every evening, and in the morning long before the dawn. For weeks the enemy had been drenching the whole area with gas — with phosgene, 'Yellow Cross II', 'mustard', 'sneezing', and 'vomiting' gas.

Early in the morning of the twenty-fourth of April there was a heavy bombardment. Where we were we had few casualties, but the thunder of doom rolled and boomed along the front.

Mid-morning grew calm. There was an insistent shelling of roads and approaches. Royal Berks. and East Lancs. came by with stretchers. They had been almost annihilated by the weight of metal. They had looked up and seen above them the iron prows of enemy tanks — used here for the first time on the Western Front — then the German masses had rolled like a Juggernaut over the remnants of the garrison. The Australian line had held, but the defenders of Villers-Bretonneux had been completely smashed. The town was lost.

At midday, horses were harnessed to our field-cookers and galloped away. We grumbled at losing our meal, then suddenly became aware that the opposite hill, was full of German infantry. Then came orders to stop all stragglers of whatever Allied nationality, and keep them with us. We were not sorry thus to reinforce our weak platoons. The Tommies proved themselves good men that night, and we thanked our stars we had escaped the hell that they had already endured. Nevertheless, we would have preferred Australians.

We heard one or two guns firing. That was some of the Australian artillery slamming at the enemy over open sights. Their fire and the existence of the long and elaborate Aubigny Line — of which the Germans already possessed the plans — alone appear to have bluffed the enemy from pushing forward then and there. If he had, there was nothing to stop him, except a few gunners. At evening we received orders to proceed to the English sector and retake the town.

From a chain of hills parallel to the Somme and south of it, an arm reaches out towards the river. Villers-Bretonneux is on a high hill at the biceps, Vaire is the elbow, Hamel is a lump on the wrist. From Villers-Bretonneux alone is there a clear view of Amiens, twelve miles away. With their overwhelming preponderance of artillery, the enemy dominated Amiens, the most vital nerve centre of the front, the most vulnerable part of the Allied spine. It was the point at which the main railway (Calais-Amiens-Paris-Verdun-Belfort) approached most nearly to the battle line. It was the point opposite which the French and British armies joined — always a vital spot, but never so much as now. Moreover, apart from ordinary dangers of a deep enemy penetration, the Germans were here within a few days march of the estuary of the Somme near Abbeville, between which and Nieuport all the British armies could be confined and wiped out in detail, leaving the flank of the French in the air, the road to Paris open. Alternatively, the British, flying along the coast from Nieuport to Havre, might perhaps have escaped that trap, and in a concave V retained touch with the French. It is hard to see how; but in any case, that line of retreat was double the distance between the Germans and Paris. Under these circumstances, the best for which we could have hoped was to lose Paris, the Channel ports, and one hundred and fifty miles of coastline fronting the south of England — and to postpone an utter defeat for a few weeks only.

A mere embarrassment near Amiens would have been sufficient to put the world in dreadful jeopardy. From Villers-Bretonneux the enemy, if he had decided to stay there, could have rendered the railway at Amiens useless and blown the city to dust — had in fact already begun to do so; for he possessed strong artillery of his own, against which we had a few — relatively very few — light guns and howitzers. But he would not have stayed on the ridge. He would have been in Amiens in two days, had not a handful of Australians flung themselves against a German corps in that black hour.

The line was stretched to breaking point, like a sheet of rubber into which a finger has been pressed. It is improbable that there were any available British reserves. Assuming their existence, it is still more improbable that they could have arrived within those terrific hours between 3.30 a.m. on the twenty-fourth and 4 a.m. on the twenty-fifth. After then, if the German forces, so numerous and so triumphant, had held the town, a larger number of divisions than could possibly have been spared would have been necessary for its recapture.

Those were the issues when less than three thousand Australians attacked three full divisions with, it was thought, eight others in reserve. (But it is said that at this crucial point of time those eight divisions were sent by the enemy to Bailleul.) Grenades and extra bandoliers were issued. We were to move at nightfall. There were successive conferences between battalion, company and platoon commanders as new facts forced the reconsideration of the plans. We set off about 10 p.m. The final dispositions were communicated to subordinate leaders while on the move. The 15th Brigade were ordered to advance on the left of the town, the 13th on the right, and by joining on the far side, to encircle it. A few English were on the western end to prevent the enemy from coming out of the town behind the striking force and cutting it off.

Along the valley we walked in single file towards Abbe Wood. We halted at the 'lie-out' position, faced left and found whatever shelter we could, for the enemy was heavily shelling this place. At length word came that all detachments were in position. Then we rose and went forward in artillery formation — lines of platoons each in a diamond with a section at the four corners. We halted at a second sunken road to spread into a double line of skirmishers, 60th on the left, 59th on the right, 57th in rear of the 59th, and some of the 58th behind the 60th. The line wheeled slightly left to avoid some hedges, then half right, the left running and stumbling. The moon sank behind clouds. There were houses burning in the town, throwing a sinister light on the scene. It was past midnight. Men muttered, 'It's Anzac Day,' smiling to each other, enlivened by the omen.

The die was now cast. It seemed that there was nothing to do but go straight forward and die hard. There was no artillery firing on either side, and we were glad. All was quiet as the grave.

Two companies of the 57th faced right to form a flank guard. They were immediately involved in fighting with German outposts. At the same time the main force, led into a bunch by converging belts of wire, became crowded and entangled in attempting to get through. It was seen. German flares of all kinds shot into the air — reds, whites, greens, bunches of golden rain. A storm of machine-gun fire came from the right and the front. Remarkably few were hit.

A snarl came from the throat of the mob, the fierce, low growl of tigers scenting blood. There was a howling as of demons as the 57th, fighting mad, drove through the wire, through the 59th, who sprang to their sides — through their enemy. The yelling rose high and passed to the 58th and 60th, who were in another mob on the left. Baying like hell hounds, they also charged. The wild cry rose to a voluminous, vengeful roar that was heard by the 13th Brigade far on the right of Villers-Bretonneux. Cheering, our men rushed straight to the muzzles of machine-guns, not troubling to take them in the flank. There was no quarter on either side. Germans continued to fire their machine-guns, although transfixed by bayonets; but though they were crack regiments of Prussian and Bavarian Guards, and though they were brave and far outnumbered the Australians, they had no chance in the wild onslaught of maddened men, who forgot no whit, in their fury, of their traditional skill. The latter were bathed in spurting blood. They killed and killed. Bayonets passed with ease through grey-clad bodies, and were withdrawn with a sucking noise. The dozen English we had with us, mere boys, and without arms till they could find a rifle, were fighting with fists and boots, happy so long as they knew where to find the Australian put in charge of them. Men were shouting, 'Coming mit a flare, Herman!' 'Vos you dere, Fritz?' Many had tallies of twenty and thirty and more, all killed with bayonet, or bullet, or bomb. Some found chances in the slaughter to light cigarettes, then continued the killing. Then, as they looked for more victims, there were cries of 'There they go, there they go!' and over heaps of big dead Germans they sprang in pursuit. One huge Australian advanced firing a Lewis gun from the shoulder, spraying the ground with lead.

It is unlikely that any of the enemy escaped their swift, relentless pursuers. They were slaughtered against the lurid glare of the fire in the town. It was man against man, and the quickest with the bayonet won. Several times Germans and Australians stood up to each other in the open and fought with grenades, the former tugging the strings in the handles of their canister bombs, then flinging them at their adversaries, the latter pulling out the pins of Mills grenades with their teeth, and bowling them overarm. One saw running forms in the dark, and the flashes of rifles, then the evil pyre in the town flared and showed to their killers the white faces of Germans lurking in shell holes, or flinging away their arms and trying to escape, only to be stabbed or shot down as they ran. Machine-gun positions were discovered burrowed under hay stacks, crammed with men, who on being found were smashed and mangled by bomb after bomb after bomb. It was impossible to take prisoners. Men could not be spared to take them to the rear; also they might easily have conducted them, in the deceiving light, to the enemy lines behind us, where erstwhile prisoners could have given their compatriots information which would have been our undoing.

We had advanced through a bottle-neck, and until

we could join with the 13th Brigade we were far inside the bottle. Here we recaptured a few wounded English who had been taken the day before. For a few minutes there was confusion. Officers were crying that we were on our objective, and ordering the men back to the trench we had passed. After a short delay, we went to the East-West Road (Warfusée-Villers-Bretonneux) a few hundred yards ahead, and sat down. We heard enemy transport rumbling over the roads. Some drove unconcernedly into our hands. They could not believe their eyes when they saw us. They were utterly ignorant of what had been happening. One would like to know what the enemy were doing all this time. These men were shot. A cart carrying a minenwerfer gun appeared. Its driver had short shrift.

There was a weird silence. An extraordinary scene then took place. 'Markers' were set out as if it were an ordinary parade ground, and a thousand men fell in in two ranks, in close order, dressed by the right, and were numbered and checked by the platoon commanders. The lurid glare of the burning houses in the town shone fitfully on the quiet ranks, where each man stood erect and steady with his rifle at the order, bloody, shining bayonet fixed, the flames reflected at intervals on all our faces.

When organisation had been rapidly induced by this extraordinary means, the line extended and went forward once more in deadly stillness. Now and again there was a shot and a wail as a German hiding in a dugout passed out, a scream and then stillness as one was found lurking in the old huts through which we were passing. Here was an abandoned British aerodrome. The great hangars bulked against the sky were black clouds passed slowly across the faces of the stars. We reached the summit of a further ridge and commenced to dig in. There was still no sign of a German counter-attack. We occupied two isolated houses.

But we were too far advanced and too far to the left. There were long undefended spaces between the English and the two flank companies left behind, and between the flank companies and us. There was also a gap on the left between the 14th and 15th Brigades. Through any of these the enemy might easily have poured and cut us off. But they did not, even though we were very few, and far 'out in the blue'.

The 57th therefore retired to the hangars, by the Warfusee Road, and the 59th passed to the right. The advance of the previous night had been about three thousand yards on an average front of six hundred — unprecedented.

Daylight found us wearily digging in. A few Germans were moving across the front, escaping from the town. We sniped them, one by one. Enemy machine-gunners dashed to the house where we had been the night before, and established their guns in a trench close by. We hit many of them, but those guns gave great trouble that day.

At seven in the morning the enemy poured a heavy and intense barrage upon us. The men were wanting sleep, but none was possible while they were stretched on that rack. Three-fourths of our total casualties were caused by the shelling. It lasted till nightfall.

Meanwhile, the two companies at the centre of the northern side of Villers-Bretonneux were pushing on steadily into the town. The Germans, at first taken unawares, were captured or killed in hundreds. There were combats from house to house. At daylight our men were advancing boldly through the streets, fired on from right and left, liable at any minute to be cut off. There were five spears pushing towards the centre of the town — two slender companies of the 57th from the left side, the English from the rear, and two detachments of the 13th Brigade from the right. All eventually met about the centre, then turning east, swept the Germans out of the town. Over a thousand Germans were captured in Villers-Bretonneux itself as they fled, the few that escaped capture or death were sniped at from our trenches on the left. Wonderful stories are told: of four men attacking over one hundred Prussian Guardsmen, fully offficered, and killing or capturing all after a stand-up fight in the open street; of a single man capturing six officers and a dozen N.C.O.s in a house within the area held at the time by the Huns. There was enormous booty in the town — field guns, field kitchens, many minenwerfers, heavy and light, hundreds of machine-guns (thirteen were found in a hedge ninety yards long and two hundred yards on the right of the place where we first encountered fire in the attack), many revolvers, technical instruments and rifles, much transport, both motor and horsed; also horses and mules, some with British markings. There were also recaptured British confidential documents, some of which had left the army printing shop within that very week.

The detachments in the town appeared on the eastern fringes at about 10 a.m., and filled the gap between the two brigades. The battle was won. A captured

German staff officer said to an Australian colonel, 'This was to have given us victory. Now I can only congratulate you on the quality of your regiments.' He was openly incredulous when told the number of the attacking force.

Several men arrived at a chateau on the outskirts of the town. It had belonged to a millionaire, and was regally furnished. There was an aviary in the grounds where birds from all parts of the world were kept. They were all dead — killed by the gas that the Germans had poured into the town before their attack. The men entered the chateau, found a billiard table, and with a typical gaiety began to play while bullets smacked through the window above their heads. They sniped the enemy through a hole in the wall between shots. One of them was pounding ragtime choruses on a grand piano.

On the Warfusee Road the men were having a bad time from shells and machine-guns. Casualties were mounting fast. Before the morning sun had completely dispelled the mists, communication from the rear was easy. Our line was on the forward slope of a ridge. There were no communication trenches. The summit behind was heavily wired. Among this wire there occurred a series of heroic acts which are no less wonderful because they are not rare.

At about 9 a.m. two runners were picking their way through the entanglement toward the front line. The mist suddenly lifted, and they were shot down by many machine-guns. One was killed, the other wounded. Throughout that day, man after man attempted to reach him. First, two stretcher-bearers succeeded in getting him upon their stretcher, when both fell, riddled with bullets; thereafter no one was able to approach within a hundred yards. The result by 4 p.m. was four killed and five wounded in attempting the rescue. Then a man, whose name is known only to his comrades, sprang from the trench, and aided by extraordinary luck, traversed untouched two hundred yards, calmly picked his way through the entanglements while bullets kicked up the dust and struck sparks from the wire. Then he carried the wounded man over the ridge. He made in all four journeys, and returned to the front line.

That night the line was consolidated under shellfire. The next day was occupied by the miserable business of sitting still and being pounded by shells, with brief intervals every four or five hours. During the following night new dispositions were made. Some of the brigade, moving from one part of the line to another, passed the English in a support trench. The latter asked them, with doubt and apprehension in their voices, if the Australians were going away. 'Yes,' was the careless answer, meaning that they themselves were vacating that particular section of the line. Gloom settled obviously on the Tommies, who apparently had learnt to lean on the strength of the Australians' arms, and having seen their work, regarded them as supermen. But when they heard that other Australians were moving into that place, the word was passed along very eagerly, and a subdued but spontaneous cheer of relief went with it, which was flattering to hear. Incidentally, the English we had 'salvaged' could only with difficulty be persuaded to leave us. They were better cared for than with their own people.

Next day the 58th and 60th advanced a little to

straighten the line.

About 6 a.m. on the twenty-seventh, after the vigil of the night, when the order to stand-down had passed along the trench, when the rum had been served and the men were beginning to crawl under their waterproof sheets for their daylight sleep, the enemy commenced to shell. Then large bodies of Germans were seen coming over the opposite hill in dense parallel columns. While two white stars, our S.O.S., were still hovering in the sky, our barrage, mostly shrapnel, descended on their masses with a deadly accuracy which counterbalanced the relative weakness of our artillery. The enemy were stopped and slaughtered in heaps while the infantry riddled the masses with lead from rifles and Lewis guns. The Germans did not reach within four hundred yards of our trench. They burrowed, shot at by our men. On the night of the twenty-ninth, we returned to our dugouts in the Aubigny line.

In a little more than three days, Villers-Bretonneux had been recaptured under circumstances which seemed not to admit the remotest chance of success, the equivalent of at least one and a half strong enemy divisions had been utterly destroyed, our position had been consolidated and held until the crucial days had passed, and a strong German attack had been completely smashed — all by the same few men.

Companies in the morning gathered round in pathetic groups of twenty or thirty, to hear the rare thanks of Field Marshall Douglas Haig in special orders of the day.

XIV

A SHOT ON THE
WRONG TARGET

We were at Cardonette, and there was to be a big divisional parade at Allonville, and every man was ordered to be on it, but Bluey and I weren't parade ground soldiers, so we thought we wouldn't go. We went instead to a little estaminet in St. Gratien, not far from the church, and sat in the back room and drank coffee with Marie and old Madame. We couldn't have *vin blanc*, we hadn't any francs. Madame would have given it to us, but one of her sons was killed in Champagne and the other was made prisoner in 1914, so it didn't seem fair.

After a while, in came a boy from the —tieth, and started talking about a motor car that old Dan (his C.O.) and Whiz-Bang (our C.O.) had both seen in Corbie, in April. He was Dan's chauffeur, and had a good job — didn't do parades, and only went as far as battalion headquarters in the line. I forgot to say that we weren't wear-

127

ing any colours, so the boy didn't know what sort of a contract he was pulling on in putting up a tale like that to us. Whiz-Bang had said 'I saw it first,' and Dan had said 'I'm senior to you,' so Dan had taken it. I looked at Bluey, but he wouldn't look at me, though I knew that there would be something doing, from the polite way he was saying, 'Is that so?' 'Did he?'

A few minutes later, Blue looked at his watch and said we'd have to be going. So we said 'Bon jour, ma'm'selle — 'day, Dig,' and closed the door behind us.

Blue dashed around the corner, I after him, wondering. In front of brigade headquarters was a lovely Mercedes car. Just then the sentry turned his back, and in a flash Blue was in the seat and I was cranking her. We drove into Cardonette. There wasn't a soul about. We left it in a shed behind the Colonel's billet. Then we hurried to the cookhouse to see if any dinner was left.

After dinner we were sent for by Puss-in-Boots, the Company Commander. Said he, 'This is the ninth occasion within the fortnight on which you have been absent without leave from parade. You are to appear before the commanding officer at 2 p.m. That is all I have to say to you. You may go.' It always took Pussy that way when he was feeling spiteful. He was studying for the ministry once.

'Well,' said the C.O., after frothing for half an hour. 'What have you to say for yourselves?'

'Oh,' said Blue, 'we were just going on parade when a bloke came along the road in your car, and . . .'

'My what?' said Whiz-Bang, considering him steadily. Blue had flicked him on the raw, but he went on serenely.

'Your car. So we nipped along to see where it went and, — and we brought it back.'

'Oh, did you. Sergeant-major, march the escort out.'

'And — er — where,' continued the C.O., fingering some papers on his desk, when we were alone, 'where is this car?'

'In the shed, sir.' Bluey opened the curtains and pointed at its shiny tonneau poking from the door.

'And don't you think … ' said Blue.

'I was wondering whether you'd … ' said I.

'H'm,' said Whiz–Bang, writing on a slip of paper, 'you've cheek enough.' He handed the slip to Blue. It read, 'Please supply one bottle whisky to bearer. (Signed) J., Lt.-Col.'

We met the Colonel at the brigade sports. He unbent so much that we wondered what was coming. He spoke of the weather, and of our prospects of winning the divisional cup. 'By the way,' he said in parting, 'next time you two men want to steal a motor car, *don't* take the Brigadier's.'

He was a sport.

On 8 August, led by the Australian and Canadian Corps, the British Army began the offensive on the Somme which ended the war. Downing here describes the fighting on the German Army's 'black day'.

XV

THE TURN OF THE TIDE
8th and 9th August 1918

PREVIOUS CONFLICTS on the Western Front had been of three different kinds. Foremost were those Allied attacks which parried the imminent destruction of our armies, or forced the enemy to relax his stranglehold. Such were Le Cateau, the battles of Ypres, both of the Marne, Verdun, the first of Villers-Bretonneux. Next were attacks which gave the Allies advantages merely, and not victory itself, such as Rheims in 1914, Neuve Chapelle, Loos, Vimy Ridge, the third of Ypres, in which the opposing forces tore each other to pieces without achieving permanent results. Lastly, there were, as on the Somme in 1916, desperate attacks with the object of disorganising a superior enemy and preventing the maturing of his plans.

According to these classifications, the first decisive victory of the Western Front was the second battle of Villers-Bretonneux. Its framework was built at Hamel. New tactics and variations of orthodox strategy were used. The 4th, 6th, 7th and 11th Brigades attacked on a three-mile front, with an intelligent impetuosity which blended well with the fighting fervour of the American elements attached to our men for schooling in modern warfare. There was fighting of the fiercest character around the German posts; there was carnage in the German line as the battle swayed backwards and forwards. The barrage crept on and on while our men rushed machine-gun after machine-gun, or sprang through the thick wire by Pear Trench and pushed their way around corners and traverses till every bay was full of German dead. The Australians fought their way through the village and over the brow of the hill, until the heights commanding a long stretch of the Somme Valley, both behind and in front, were ours.

Meanwhile, in order to ensure their comrades an easier task at Hamel, the 15th Brigade had made a feint attack; in front of Ville-sur-Ancre and Morlancourt, on the left. This operation was, necessarily, not so fully equipped as the main attack, and the proportion of casualties was fairly heavy; but the objectives were taken and held; and the attack succeeded in drawing thither large forces of the enemy, for the 58th Battalion encountered and defeated no less than three times the number of Germans than it expected to meet. To their aid came some of the 57th who had swum the Ancre under heavy fire. For a time the 59th and 60th were held up in violent fighting, but at length the whole brigade forged forward to the consummation of a victory over heavy odds, a victory equal in quality to that on the right.

In the succeeding days our men were permitted to make marauding forays on their own initiative within the enemy lines; to engage in manhunts in the crops which covered no man's land; to creep up on German posts hidden in the uncut corn; and to lie in wait for parties of Germans and kill three or four times their number — 'gentlemanly affairs by a sergeant and a few friends'. They went out in twos and threes, and not a night went by without a strong enemy patrol, generally of ten or twelve men, being driven back to its trench with loss. The result of these freelance enterprises was that casualties were inflicted on the enemy, his trenches were entered, his wire cut, his machine-gun and minenwerfer positions located; his ration parties were fired on, he was denied the information to be gained by patrols, and his men became jumpy and worried. Shelling was heavy on both sides.

After a week of this, the division was relieved from the line and marched openly to the suburbs of Amiens, by easy stages. It was no sooner there than it returned, by forced marches under cover of night, towards Abbe Wood, a mile behind the town, now a dreary ruin, of Villers-Bretonneux.

The battalions passed through the moonlit streets of empty Amiens, beneath the black shadow of its cathedral's towering mass. The city, so crowded, so gay, so prosperous, so full of mediaeval charm when last we had seen it, was dead and empty. No bells of tramcars clanged in the shadows of the steep and winding streets; no lights blazed in the cafes; no brightly coloured crowds circulated between the guildhalls and the chapels, or through the flowers in the Place Gambetta.

Over the paving stones, across the bridges, the hard, lean men marched in silence through that dead husk. No man spoke to his fellow until the city was far behind. They were impressed (whom it was hard to impress) by the sadness of the place. They felt themselves to be the instruments of its liberation, though they had been told little of the coming battle. When far into the country, someone started one of the absurd and whimsical marching songs the troops affected.

Every night the cobblestones of all the roads of all that countryside resounded with the clatter and the roll of many parallel streams of transport. The highways were crowded with tanks, with field guns, with motor lorries carrying war material of every kind, with nine-point-two howitzers, with gargantuan siege guns whose mammoth barrels were borne on tractors, while their bodies rolled behind them on their giant iron wheels — all going the one way, making the hillsides vibrate with their thunder. Among these packed columns, strings of horsemen and of laden infantry wound their way.

It began to rain. The boom and flickering of guns were nearer and nearer. At length there were shellbursts on the road, a derelict tank, a dead mule or two. We had marched twenty miles.

That night we lay in the rain, on the side of the railway embankment, under heavy shell-fire. It was very cold. We wondered if the day of the attack would be dry. Well we knew the result of mud, even of an inch.

The next day was dull and lowering. Shells thumped and crashed in Abbe Wood and along the embankment. There was a tunnel a hundred feet long where the road and the mass of traffic of all kinds that it bore passed beneath the railway. This was crammed with men. Outside were whipping showers and flying steel. Motor lorries, ambulances, guns, wagons and limbers dashed to and fro among the shells.

Details of the attack, the hour, the methods, were wrapped in mystery. The previous day we had said 'tomorrow'; we were still there, tired, and depressed by the weather. A few officers and N.C.O.s went to the front line to view the ground. They returned round-eyed with wonder. The woods on the right were full of Canadians. Canadians? We thought they were at Arras. We were glad to have them with us. We had known them at Passchendaele. There were heavy guns almost in the front line, ready to fire when the advance went beyond range of the barrage artillery. They were so camouflaged that one could touch them yet scarcely see them. Villers-Bretonneux was full of tanks of all kinds and for diverse purposes. A stray shell fell among some of these and set a number on fire. There was a column of smoke and the crackle of burning ammunition in the town. Did the enemy know of the coming attack?

We ate, dug, slept, thought, played cards, wrote letters, scattered from the shells. Our preparations were complete. Grenades, rifle grenades, ammunition bandoliers, extra water bottles, spades, picks, signal rockets, extra rations, wire cutters — all the weighty war museum that an infantryman carries into action — were issued. Trench maps and aeroplane photographs of the terrain were distributed.

The forthcoming battle, if all went well, was to be one which no adventurous soul could wish to miss. For the first time an old aspiration was to be realised. All the Australians were gathered together and we had the advantage of being with men on whom, above all oth-

135

ers, we knew we could rely, and who would rely on us. The active and spirited comradeship of Australians in the field formed bonds stronger than the ties of a Highland clan. It was our greatest asset and our strongest recommendation. The event had been long hoped for. There were high prospects of a sweeping and brilliant success. On our right were to be Canadians and French; on the left, the Scotch. For all of these our rivalry was tempered by a strong esteem. There were also some splendid divisions of English.

Experiments in tactics made at Hamel were here elaborated. Supply tanks carrying ammunition, rations and necessary materials of all kinds were allocated. There were also the new Mark V fighting tanks, whippet tanks of a maximum speed of sixteen miles an hour, and armoured cars for use on roads and hard ground, detailed to exploit our successes and to pursue the enemy. Other tanks were to be used for making barbed wire entanglements in front of our final positions. Aeroplanes also were to be used to carry supplies and to save the infantry in this way from all avoidable wastage and fatigue. Observation squadrons were to direct the men on the ground towards any opportunities of greater success that might be presented. Swarms of fighting planes were to sweep the enemy out of the skies. Every available gun except those hidden near the line was to be used. While some smothered the enemy artillery, others were to flatten the villages where enemy headquarters were known to be, thus paralysing the enemy command, and to encircle with a barrage all places where there were likely to be reserves of troops, and either annihilate them or prevent their use. The bulk of our batteries were to lay down a terrific barrage on the enemy trenches. One-tenth of the shells were to contain chemicals forming dense clouds of smoke which would screen our movements. When the advance went beyond reach of the rear artillery, the hidden guns were due to open, while the remainder moved forward.

The first objective was called the Blue Line, and was just under three miles from our original front.

The second was another four and a half, and named the Red Line. There was a further objective, the Exploiting Line, to be reached if it could be done without undue loss. At a distance behind the last wave of infantry, horsed and motor ambulances followed the roads. Regimental stretcher-bearers were ordered not to carry the wounded after we passed the first German trench system, but to bandage them and leave them for the ambulances.

In the darkness of the night of the seventh of August we followed country cart tracks and brick-strewn roads through the melancholy ruins of Villers-Bretonneux to the front trenches. There we found our guide tapes and followed them as the enemy was firing bursts of bullets. By the small hours of morning we were spreading along the front, in no man's land.

The 2nd Division was ahead, lying out. We clattered and stumbled and clinked to our places behind them, in a long single line without intervals, for there was no time to move in small groups. Then shells began bursting around us. They were mostly 'whizz-bangs' with '106' fuses — instantaneous caps which caused the shell to burst without penetrating the ground — 'daisy-clippers' which flung the fragments outwards, not upwards.

The fragments scored hundreds of long straight radiating lines in the grass and could cut a man's legs from under him. We were caught in the barrage. We huddled in shellholes, crowded together. We spread out as soon as there was opportunity. German machine-guns were firing low. Bullets whizzed and cracked as we ran from cover to cover. Red-hot, they ricocheted between us, lolloping past like red beetles. Platoon sergeants searched the ground in the darkness. They found an old trench (probably one we had dug ourselves, on April the twenty-fifth) and got their men under its cover. At length the shelling slackened.

Remarkably few men had been hit. But how much did the enemy know? Later we learnt from prisoners that our attack was expected to be made four days after the real date. The Germans intended to attack that very morning and forestall us. This was why so many of them were encountered in their trenches. We lay on the white tapes marking our assembly line behind the 2nd Division. We looked at our watches from time to time. The men fidgetted. Two thirty-four — four forty-five — seven to five — five to five — a minute to go — ten seconds — ZERO TIME.

As though a flaming dawn had been flung into the sky, the whole world flared behind us. There was a titanic pandemonium of ten thousand guns. We shouted to each other, but we could not hear our own voices, buried beneath colossal ranges of sound. The lighter, more metallic notes of thousands of field guns were blended in one long-drawn chord. The hoarse and frantic rumble of the sixty-pounders, the long naval guns, the great howitzers, was like the rapid burring of a thousand drums. The light pieces were like trombones, for there were no individual sounds except the bark, bark, bark of an eighteen-pounder battery close behind us. And always, thrutter-thrutter-thrutter went the heavies.

White smoke curled over us and hid the flaming skies. There was a thrumming as of gigantic bumble bees, and a low chug-chug-chug, as the ugly noses of the tanks poked through the mist above us. We hastily scattered from the path of one and found ourselves almost beneath others. They went forward in a line, scarcely thirty yards between them. They were in scores, and their vibrations sounded through the fog from every side, like another layer of sound on the bellow of the guns.

Then a rattling of machine-guns told us that the lads in front were at grips with the enemy. We heard the sound of many bombs, German and British, both unmistakable. Vainly we tried to pierce the white blankets of smoke, to see how they were faring. Our hearts were with them. Good men were going out, two hundred yards away. Walking wounded came back through the curling tongues of mist, and gloomy strings of prisoners. Pleasantries, but not bitter or insulting, were flung to the latter, who either ignored them, or turned with wan smiles.

'How are they going?'

'In their second line.'

This from the stretcher-bearers, carrying severely wounded. They disappeared in the mist. The noise of fighting was buried deeper and deeper in the fog. It was now far ahead.

At six o'clock we rose and went forward. We passed

many German and Australian dead, bulky heaps in the fog. The ground was pitted and churned, but the rain had held off. It was after the hour of sunrise, though little light could pierce the smoke-pall. We lost all idea of time and space. We hurried forward, fearful lest we should be late at our places. Actually we went far too fast. We were due to reach the Blue Line at twenty past eight, three and one-third hours after zero. There we were to 'leap frog' through the 2nd Division. There was a rattle of musketry, and bombs were bursting once more. Bullets zipped among us. We made our way forward, and joined some of the leading waves. In this particular place they were held up by some obstinate posts. We worked around the flanks of a trench where the Germans were. Suddenly a machine-gun opened fire on us, not fifty yards away. We had run straight into an outpost. We dropped and opened fire at the place. Then five figures, huge in the mist, rose and ran. We shot at them. One seemed to stumble. One fell. A moan came through the opaque vapours. The others disappeared. There were violent flurries of fire from different places, now and again. The bullets zipped and swished in clusters, and cracked in the air. Several of our men crumpled into heaps. Others were wounded in arms and legs, or lay groaning on the ground. A slight breeze blew some of the smoke away. We were looking down a trench. A hundred yards along there were Germans in it. We dropped to cover and opened rapid fire.

Then the boys of the 7th Brigade sprang like lions at their enemies, and the smoke pall covered them. We heard mad cheering, shots, a gurgling cry. Incidents like this kept recurring on our way to the Blue Line — our first objective, five thousand yards from the 'lie-out' position. We were still anxious about the weather, but hopeful. Suddenly we burst out of the mist, and joy! There was a cloudless sky and bright sunshine. The stars in their courses had fought for us — at first, days of bad weather, to hide our preparations, then a dark night, then a dry, sunny day. We were beyond the region of shellholes, on a hard road, among crops. Larks rose singing from the corn. We sat in an empty trench.

Our shells were still roaring through the air, but falling far away, on the villages. Here it was peaceful as a rural Sunday, except on the right, where the Canadians were having trouble with some difficult country, copses and farms. They were very anxious to beat us to our objectives, and had made many wagers with us. By seven o'clock we were on the Blue Line, an hour and twenty minutes before the scheduled time. Our men were mingled with all the successive waves of our precursors, and it took half an hour to reorganise them. Some of the 2nd Division had already pushed a little way ahead, and were sending back prisoners. Apart from these, there was not a German in sight. They were all dead or prisoners, or had fled. We expected to meet a newly formed enemy line further on. We hurriedly breakfasted, anxious to keep the enemy on the run. Shortly before the time appointed for the second stage of the battle, the Canadians took Marcelcave, immediately across the railway from where we were, and all was ready for us to go forward. We had watched them at work — encircling villages, storming strong posts and fighting through woods. They had a rough time, for the difficulties of their terrain were often great, but they were good men. In the ancient Homeric style they were led in person by their colonel, and their chaplain accompanied them! We were often able to assist them when we were farther forward than they, by firing into the backs of the enemy across the railway line.

Aeroplanes were wheeling and swooping, far forward in the sky. There was a fight between two planes and five. The two fell in flames, almost together, leaving long, perpendicular trails of black smoke. Several of our tanks were lying derelict in front. One was burning. A few long-distance shells began to fall close by. Nevertheless, except for the fighting at dawn, it was more like a picnic than a battle. There were few of the usual depressing concomitants of a major action — rain, tumbled waves of earth, enemy barrages, mutilation.

At twenty past eight all was ready for the second stage of the operation. We assembled in front of the Blue Line in four waves, each consisting of a double line of dots, each dot a little group or section of men in single file, each group placed on the forward and reverse angles of the teeth of an imaginary saw, in a slanting, zig-zag pattern. There was a space laterally between the sections of thirty yards; and between each successive section it was two hundred. This is technically known as 'artillery formation', because, to do serious harm, a shell must fall very close by the men, and no single shrapnel burst can damage more than one section. Hence it gives the maximum of protection against shelling. Also, on encountering machine-gun fire, it is easy to extend from this formation into a single line.

We moved off. Most of the German artillery had been smothered by our barrage. Except for a few snipers and machine-guns, there was little resistance. We saw bodies of retreating Germans in the distance, chased by our shrapnel. The tanks affiliated to us bore our regimental colour patches painted on them. They crawled through us, then zig-zagged forward across our front. We worked through copses, crops and trenches, enveloped factories and farms. A few shells skimmed over us, flying very low at a prodigious speed, with a swish and a bang. We were buffeted by their wind. One dropped short and burst under the forepart of a tank. It lifted sideways, settled forward, and stopped. The door opened and two or three men ran out, dragging a wounded man. One went back, recovered a Lewis gun, and hoisted a yellow flag, the 'knocked-out' signal. We were behind a cemetery. On the hill beyond, a German battery of high velocity five-point-nine guns was blazing at us, point blank, the muzzles depressed below horizontal. We ran toward them, the shells roaring among us. When we were within two hundred yards, they ceased fire. We swarmed into the gun pits. The gunners climbed out of a deep dugout, holding up their hands and shaking their fingers. We passed on.

Thereafter it was fairly plain sailing. Whenever we found ourselves in trouble, we signalled to the tanks, and they turned towards the obstacle. Then *punk-crash*, *punk-crash!* As their little toy guns spoke and their little, pointed shells flew, another German post was blown to pieces. *Punk-crash!* A brick wall tottered and crumbled amid a cloud of red dust. We passed the place. The machine-gun and its crew were crushed and still. A rabbit jumped up and bounded away. With joyful shouts a hundred men started in pursuit. *Crack-swish*, *crack-swish*,

swish. The air was full of bullets. The men left the rabbit and advanced by sporadic dashes, then gathered themselves for a final rush. They bayoneted the machine-gunners, then passed on. There were more bullets, but mostly high. The Canadians were in difficulties again. We climbed the railway embankment and lay down. Below us was a ravine. We fired into the Germans' backs, for we had forged ahead of our neighbours. The trouble was being caused by a thick wood (Bois Picuret), strongly held. We pumped lead into the trees. Half a mile away, close to the far fringe of the wood, some men were dashing towards the enemy. Three or four dropped sprawling. A tank trundled ridiculously to the rescue. We lay and watched like spectators at a play, in a breathless silence. The tank began shooting six-pound shells and tap-tapping with a machine-gun. One of our boys laughed aloud from sheer joy. 'Oh, the bonnie little tank!' A German gun barked at her. Missed! The tank replied with all her weapons. Then she turned, and firing only the left gun, manoeuvred to a position where the Germans could not fire on her without moving the field gun bodily. The tank's shells were at least preventing its enemy from doing good shooting, for four German shots missed. Then one fell close to her tail. She plunged and shuddered, but did not stop. After that the field piece did not fire again. Its crew must have been killed. We could not see. The tank halted and flew the yellow flag, but she had done her work and done it well. Germans came running out of the back of the wood, in a mob. We put a burst of machine-gun fire into them from our commanding position. The survivors surrendered. Canadian infantry emerged from the wood and took charge of them.

For miles and miles infantry were everywhere advancing, dotted over hill and dale on either hand as far as the eye could see. Bayonets grouped and glinted in the charge as a battalion swarmed to the storming of a town miles away. Here and there thick columns of smoke and spluttering explosions told that the enemy dumps were burning. Red roofs and white walls trembled in the hot sunshine where villages drowsed beneath their lichened elms; the crops were lemon green, the pastured hillsides of a richer verdure; double rows of poplars shadowed the long straight roads. We went through a dump of engineers' material and captured some lurking Germans. We found an abandoned battery of howitzers. We passed a derelict armoured train on a loop siding. It carried a huge gun (probably the 'Bertha' later exhibited in Paris). We had no time to examine it, for a machine-gun in a hedge was firing at us. The gunners left it and fled.

We passed Wiencourt on our right. One of our planes landed in our midst. The machine was riddled with bullet holes. We gave the pilot goodday and went on. He nodded cheerfully and lit a cigarette. We were now very weary.

We entered the part of Guillaucourt on the left of the railway. *Jaegers* sniped us from a tower. It seemed a large town. There was a big church with a steeple of sixteenth century Spanish architecture. There was shooting in the streets by men dropping on one knee, and we were firing and being fired at from windows. The tanks rumbled through the town firing left and right till the enemy poured out of the houses and surrendered in droves.

Through a marsh the going was heavy. We pushed on. There was heavy fighting for Harbonnieres, a mile on the left. Tanks were circling about it, and infantry were running forward. The tanks on our front were busy with some enemy posts. Then for a time we had to overcome a strong resistance.

Cavalry rode over the hills behind and trotted among us. Then they went through in close formation. Our own shells were falling among us. That was because we were ahead of time, so we slackened the pace. We came upon an old trench made by the French in 1915. This was our day's objective, the Red Line. We had advanced eight miles.

Whippet tanks came through, and armoured cars were running along the roads. Around a copse on our left front horsemen came galloping, and disappeared among some hedges. They returned with large parties of prisoners.

Our artillery was following. Australian batteries trotted into position in a ravine behind us. On the opposite hill, about a mile away, Germans were swarming around a train. It slowly drew away, then, gathering speed, disappeared, leaving great puffs of steam. A second train began to move, then stopped. Men on horseback were riding round it. It disgorged a crowd of men. Our cavalry had it. Australian Light Horse patrols were riding swiftly all over the country. The whippets entered a wood and a village far in front.

The men were very exhausted by the labours of the last few days. We lay that night among the long weeds and the wildflowers that grew in the old trench. Until daylight, we patrolled the front in turns, but all was quiet. The battalion transport brought hot food. We were shelled at extreme range all night.

Next day (August the ninth) some local advances were undertaken. We moved forward under hedges and banks, along trenches and sunken roads; a 'peaceful penetration' of a thousand yards, without a barrage and under machine-gun fire. But casualties were slight, and positions commanding the opposite slopes were secured. The enemy retired sullenly, a little farther.

Where we were all was quiet, except a few machine-guns and snipers, but on our left there was a counter-attack. A mass of Germans rolled forward. Then the Australians climbed from their trench and rushed to meet it at the bayonet's point. The enemy wavered, turned their backs and swayed in confusion. When our men were almost on them they ran forward with hands uplifted. Far away, our shrapnel was bursting in black and white puffs over Lihons Wood.

At 11.00 a.m. a new attack was made along the whole line. The 1st Division, come newly from the North, but intact so far as recent fighting was concerned, was coming through. If it could not arrive in time we were to go over. It was not a pleasant prospect, for we were tired, and our artillery was not yet present in full strength. We had lost half our number in casualties, and had already been involved in three phases of the present battle.

The time drew near. We were twice ordered to prepare to attack, twice the advance was postponed. At last the 58th and 60th, who had been following us through the fighting, lined our trench. Over they went, at first in a line, but a storm of bullets forced them to advance 'by sectional rushes'. Groups of seven or eight men here and there began dashing forward in short spurts, while their mates tried to keep down the Germans' heads with covering fire. Men were dropping fast. They advanced about nine hundred yards, and came to grips with the German posts. There was hot fighting. We were mounting the parapet to follow, when a runner hurried through the trench. 'From Captain —— to all platoon sergeants — Don't go over.' We wondered. Then we looked behind us.

And there was the 1st Division, in artillery formation, dotted over the ridge a mile behind. The waves in their regular patterns stretched backwards for thousands of yards, and sideways for miles. No one who has not seen a full division advancing 'in depth' down the slopes of the hills can know the majesty of the sight. On they came. They passed over us. It was twenty minutes before the last wave went through.

'Best of luck, 8th Battalion.'

'Thanks, boys.'

Their fresh faces contrasted with ours, which were unshaven, and grimy and wan. They strode on, and on, and on. Shrapnel eddied and flashed and puffed above them, bullets ripped through their formation. As one man fell, another stepped into his place, without slackening, without hurrying, outwardly calm.

They extended into single lines and swept forward to Lihons Wood. Then they advanced by short rushes. We saw them charge with the bayonet, far away. They reached the Wood, tiny dots, as tiny as when we first saw them, a long way behind. Parties of men came and went with stretchers. Batches of prisoners shambled through. Motor ambulances rolled along the road by our trench as the sun was setting. A frog croaked from a weedy ditch. A bird began its song.

XVI

SUPPER FOR FOUR

W<small>E HAD</small> just been into Amiens to hire some costumes for the battalion concert, and had spent the last of our gilt. It was four days from payday, so we mooched round the estaminets, but nobody shouted. At closing time Blue said, 'Come along and see Louise.'

We looked through the window before we went in. There were *beaucoup* bottles of champagne on the table, and places set for four. There was chicken in a dish on the stove.

Said Blue — 'Now I wonder which particular Lothario is butting in here.'

We went round the back and opened the door. 'Louise,' said Blue, 'you're *pas bon*.' (This was only the Lingua Franca of the troops. He could speak French like a native, when he wanted to — had two months in a French hospital, after Cape Helles.)

She flew to his side — 'Bluee, ah Bluee!' A small hand slid into his. He looked down at her, surly. We heard the front door open and heavy footsteps in the hall.

'Who's in there, then?'

She shrugged her shoulders. 'Officiers, mais que veux tu? Eet ees business an' t'ey pay maman, an' what can we do?'

'Berthe inside?' said I. We went in. We had a glimpse through the door at the party, reflected in a mirror. Berthe came out.

'Blue,' said I, 'the Lord hath delivered them into our hand.' We told the girls their part of the plan. Then we hurried by a short cut to our billet.

The party went well — up to a certain point. The girls were in high spirits, but avoided each other's eyes. Officer Puss-in-Boots made love to each in turn. Officer Bully made terrific inroads on the chicken.

There was a rap on the door, and a loud voice, 'Ouvrez, s'il vous plait.'

Les gendarmes! There were horrified whispers. The matter was serious for all, but for Madame it meant the estaminet being put out of bounds, because raids by the gendarmes were made in conjunction with our Military Police, and neither party would fail to report the case, not knowing enough of the other's language to work any schemes.

Louise hid the champagne under the table, while Berthe made the two lie on a bed in the next room, and covered them with a quilt.

'Damn this,' whispered Bully, 'why did she insist on putting us here?'

'For Heaven's sake shut up. You're making the bed

creak.'

'What's he saying?'

'O Lord,' groaned the other, 'he's found your cap.'

The 'gendarme' entered the bedroom. Behind him came Berthe, looking distressed. Peeping from the coverlet, Puss-in-Boots caught a glimpse of an arm bearing a Military Policeman's badge in the parlour. The gendarme, his huge moustache moving like the antennae of a suspicious moth, pulled off the coverlet. Puss and Bullybeef rose, angry and sheepish, straightening their collars and slapping at the fluff on their clothes. The gendarme turned angrily on Berthe. 'Hein! Voila! Hein!' spreading out his palms in a gesture expressing condemnation, exposition and interrogation, and which included Berthe, Madame, the two officers and the parlour. 'Hein! Gardez! Hein!' Then he inundated the girls with a torrent of recrimination. He portentously pulled out a notebook and strode into the parlour, Berthe following.

Louise entered the bedroom, from the kitchen, pointing to the open window. 'Allez, allez!' she whispered. They went, walking in the shadow of a hedge.

That evening we had champagne and chicken for supper, Berthe and Louise and Blue and I.

At the concert, our song, 'The Bold Gendarme', made a tremendous hit, especially when Blue waggled his false moustache. I suppose the regimental Military Police enjoyed it most, but I know who didn't enjoy it at all.

XVII

PÉRONNE AND MONT ST. QUENTIN
31st August to 5th September 1918

ON THE twenty-third of August the 1st Division, 'leap-frogging' the 5th at Proyart, made a victorious drive to the depth of many miles, storming, on its way, villages heavily fortified and strongly held, Chuignes, Chuignolles, and the rest. The 3rd and 4th Divisions, advancing in conformity with the 1st, captured the important town of Bray, and passed beyond it.

The 1st Division was south of the Somme, the 3rd and 4th were north of it. From Corbie and Hamel the direction of the advance was upstream, parallel to the Somme, as far as Péronne, where that river turns sharply to the right towards Ham, in the shape of a gallows-tree.

Péronne appeared a hard nut to crack. In front was a high rampart, a citadel, a river; on the right was a long marsh, with an arm reaching backwards and partly encircling the town; on the left were the heights of Mont St. Quentin; behind were wooded hills; a rampart and a moat, broad and deep, protected the landward side. Among the marshes on the left was the village of Doingt. The entire sector was held by divisions of picked men who had volunteered from all the German armies 'to meet the Australians'.

French experts, relying on their experience of the place in 1916, held that the river could not be crossed in less than a month. The English believed that it might be done in a fortnight. The Australians were over in three days, and in six had taken every position. After the success of the 1st Division had driven the Germans south of the Somme from their chain of fortifications, it was easy for the advanced brigades of the 2nd and 5th to push the enemy to the crossbar of the gallows, the river at Péronne, where for a time he was in danger of being jammed — against an obstacle which a large body of men could cross only by the aid of broad and numerous bridges, as later we found to our cost.

And so, from the green garden country around Lihons and Chipilly, treading on their heels all the way, we had pushed the Huns to the shell-pocked battlefields over which the French had fought for the same objectives in 1916, and whose desolation was now partly hidden by a rank, tangled mat of weeds. The advanced guards of the Australians met and broke a stiffening resistance in the last few miles. The enemy was fighting for breath, fighting for time to get across the marshes of the Somme to his prepared positions on the other side. There were some violent little struggles for a trench here, a hilltop there, a farmhouse somewhere else. When our skirmishers reached the river, the Huns had succeeded, only just in time, in withdrawing beyond it.

But the swift fighting of the A.I.F. had at least prevented the maturing of his plans.

There were no crossings, for all the bridges had been blown up. The whole length of the river reaches was commanded by, and under the direct observation of, the German artillery across the valley. A deep swift river ran before us, between high-built banks. Beyond were spread broad swamps, ten feet deep, muddy at the bottom, and matted with reeds and tussocks through which no boat, no swimmer, could possibly force a way. They varied in breadth from five to eight hundred yards. The opposite shore was alive with machine-guns. The forests on the hills behind were full of batteries which shot at everything that moved in our trenches.

Many attempts were made to get across. If they had succeeded, the battle of Mont St. Quentin might not have been necessary. It was found impossible, however, for engineers to throw bridges across so wide a space, or under so heavy a rain of shells. A few narrow duckboard paths, twenty inches wide and built on high trestles, were indeed discovered; but they were death traps. Patrols, wading hither and thither on the edge of the marsh, found and followed them among the tussocks until, on turning a corner, the men found themselves in the face of enemy machine-guns, set by design to sweep the track at point-blank range. There were many gallant but futile deeds — when, attempting to push forward at any cost, or dashing into showers of bullets to the aid of comrades lying wounded and limp upon the boards with their bodies hung half in the water, our men walked one by one to death, and fell in heaps on those narrow wandering causeways, or tumbled into the marsh and sank beneath its rippling surface, as the bullets splashed in the water or struck splinters from the duckboards. It was a hopeless business. Meanwhile, the 3rd Division, in triumph from the taking of Bray, swept to the foot of the northern slopes of Mont St. Quentin, a point level with the two divisions within the river's angle. Under cover of this move the 5th Brigade (2nd Division), in a detour of several miles, moved to the left, crossed the Somme and drove forward till it lay on the right of the 3rd Division. Then the 14th Brigade, by the aid of covering fire from the 5th, was enabled to cross the river on the right of the latter. This movement threatened the German flank and permitted the 15th Brigade in turn to force its way over the stream and into Péronne.

Thus a twofold movement took place. Along the entire Australian front the brigades sidestepped, piecemeal, from right to left. At the same time the whole line, with its right at Péronnè as a hinge, swung across the river like a gate.

On the thirty-first of August, immediately after crossing the river, the 5th Brigade attacked the Mont. Ringed with trenches from base to summit, its approaches swept by a tornado of bullets and lashed by zones of bursting shells, the hill was now, even as it had been during the first years of the war, one of the most formidable positions on the Western Front. But the 5th Brigade, in spite of heavy punishment, and in spite of a violent and determined resistance, rolled up the hillside, rolled back, gathered itself together, and at the end of a day of terrible fighting, held all but the topmost trenches.

On its right a part of the 14th Brigade attacked a

maze of trenches hidden in Anvil Wood and protected by entanglements laid in broad belts in the fields and wreathed among the undergrowth. After a furious fight in which the attackers were badly mauled, our men penetrated the wood; and in doing so the 53rd Battalion was almost exterminated.

On the next day, while the 10th and 11th attacked on the left of Mont St. Quentin, the 6th Brigade, although encountering a violent barrage, captured the summit, repulsed local counter-attacks, and consolidated the position. At the same time the 15th attacked Péronne.

On the front of that brigade the town walls stood in some places sheer from the water, and in others had at their foot only a narrow space of ground. Our men, having gained possession of some houses on the south-west bank, at length, by means of broken bits of bridges and the pontoons of the engineers, began to cross, struggling with the chilly river as the enemy poured fire into them. But the Germans were themselves receiving enfilade fire from the 14th Brigade; and at length their machine-guns slackened sufficiently for the stormers to gain a footing on the farther bank. Once there, they had to fight for their lives, for there could be no retreat. So they pushed their way at the bayonet's point into the town. The black pile of the citadel with its rugged basalt walls was encircled, and its garrison withdrew. The struggle passed deeper and deeper into Péronne.

By dawn on the 2nd of September the 58th, 59th and 60th were all fighting through the rubble-strewn streets and the shattered houses. On the same morning the 7th Brigade swept down the farther slopes of Mont St. Quentin, and the 14th Brigade, in the centre of the battle, attacked between the 7th and 15th. Little by little the enemy was driven through the town, till the furthermost battlements were ours, and the Huns withdrew to the woods and marshes which reached back from the moat towards the hills. The enemy vented his wrath in a frenzy of shelling, and set the town on fire.

Two miles on the right the 57th was still making strenuous efforts to find a way through the inexorable lagoons. It was now taken from its fruitless task and sent to relieve the sorely battered 58th, for the town had been dearly won. Pursued by bursting shells, the companies followed the river from Barleux, and bullets whizzed among them all the way.

We came to a place where the ends of a shattered bridge sloped into the water, its broken back deep beneath the surface. We crossed on two planks that swayed with our footsteps in the dark. The stream rushed and whirled and beat against the shattered masonry and twisted iron, roaring over the sunken blocks, raising itself in a crested wave whose whiteness was seen beneath, faintly in the gloom, as we shuffled carefully on that frail pathway, laden as we were. The planks were very narrow. The stream was deep, but we could see neither the water nor our own uncertain feet. Encumbered and weary, our rifles swaying on their slings from our shoulders, we crossed in single file. Bullets were flying in the air, shells were crashing on the banks and flinging bricks into the water, or bursting beneath the surface, each with a muffled boom and a shower of spray. A slip meant death in the waters.

In two hours we were all across and winding through the town in single file. It was in flames. A moan came from a shattered house as we passed. A beam fell amid a shower of sparks, and something burst into flame; then, as the walls within were lit by its yellow glare we heard a scream in the gutted rooms and a voice that babbled in German. We hurried on, for our mates in front were hard beset: but still we heard with horror that shrieking wretch behind us.

We saw the orange flashes and heard the bursting of shells among the houses on every side. We climbed through a breach in a wall, stumbled among the heaps of bricks, emerged in a courtyard, and turned a corner where a man was posted to point out the way. Singly we dashed across a street swept with bullets from the direction of the marsh. Heavy stones were thumping on the ground. A shell burst on the string of hurrying men, and a body with broken limbs hurtled through the air like a rag doll, thudded against a wall and dropped to the ground, inert. We turned a corner, crossed the square of the town, and saw the moon through the broken tracery of the tall windows of the church. We mounted stone steps, entered a carved archway, and passed through a narrow corridor of stone into a courtyard, as the clouds rolled over the moon. At length we came to the ramparts, crossed the moat and reached the trenches of the 58th. The garrison moved to the rear, and we spread along the line. Before us was a little dry land, then a marsh with trees growing in the water, about three hundred yards wide. Beyond the marsh was a railway embankment twenty or thirty feet high. It was held by the enemy.

All that night we patrolled the front in small parties, searching for paths in the water, looking for the troops on right and left (for there were many gaps in the line), seeking the Huns. All the next day was spent in the same manner. Sometimes we encountered German posts among the trees, sometimes unseen enemies followed us with bullets as we moved among the undergrowth.

There was a peat-cutter's hut in a thicket. Many times we had passed within full view of it. A couple of men, wandering casually with their rifles slung across their backs, entered the hut in search of 'souvenirs'. They found, within, a crowd of Germans, some asleep, others playing cards, and a number cleaning the parts of a machine-gun. One of the Australians quickly picked up a clod of earth and threw it into the mechanism, so that the Huns were unable to put the gun together, and the two men got away.

All day the enemy filled our line with bursting shells. It was not until night that by means of 'fighting patrols' and by gradually working forward in little nibbles from post to post, we advanced the line to the embankment, which the enemy vacated on seeing our approach. Beyond was a dense wood. We crossed the railway and searched among the trees, creeping along dark paths in single file, running, bent low, across the moonlit glades, beating the forest for our human quarry, thinking the trees were full of unseen eyes, expecting every minute machine-guns to flash and rattle in our very faces, every sense on the alert lest we should walk into an ambush. But the Huns had gone.

It was dawn when we passed through the wood and reached a trench. We followed its windings and found the Germans in posts in the trench. We attacked them with bombs, driving them helter-skelter towards Doignt, between us and the Somme.

Doignt was separated from Péronne by that arm of marsh previously referred to. The enemy in the village was now inside the angle of the river and this marsh, and by pushing sufficiently far along the trench we would have cut off his retreat had he not, seeing the object of our movement, evacuated the position. The Germans hurried through a sap at right angles to our own, and we hurried to meet them. There was a race to the intersection of the two trenches. But the enemy was nearer, and we were in time only to engage his rearguard in a bomb fight, to capture some stragglers, and to snipe at the main body as it withdrew.

But Doingt, the last outpost of Péronne, was ours. This was on September the fifth. The enemy did not cease to retreat until the advanced positions of the Hindenburg Line were reached and the Germans, followed by our brigades, had been hounded to Templeux. And that was the beginning of the end.

XVIII

SOME CHARACTERISTICS

ONE MUST beware of partiality in speaking of one's own. Panegyrics rather bored the Australian and excited his suspicion, for they were usually followed by a request to do an extra 'stunt'. Secretly, of course, he was often gratified, for he was in many ways a simple soul and very human.

Probably the fiercest fighter of the war was the French-Canadian. He was the only one who kept unblunted the keen edge of his blood lust through all the deadening hammerings of the long campaigns. After him in this one respect are ranked the Australian, the Highlander of the 51st Division, and the English-speaking Canadian, all fairly equal.

The highest peaks of heroism tower so far above us ordinary men that it is impossible to make comparisons. Therefore, we dare not say that the Australian is braver in the average than the English, the French or the Germans. The following is an extract from an offficial report of what some Tommies did: —

'The subsequent story is so brimful of heroism that it deserves to take its place in English history for all time, and to be a proud day in the lives of all those splendid British soldiers who by their single-hearted devotion to duty saved ... a catastrophe ...

'The rearguard, assisted by machine-guns, held off the whole of the enemy's attack until the main portion of the battalion was fully organised, and they died to a man with their face to the enemy.

'Of the heroism of the rearguard it is difficult to speak. Captain Stone and Lieut. Bezencry, although ordered to withdraw to the main line, elected to remain with the rearguard. The rearguard was soon fighting with bayonet, bullet, and bomb to the last. There was no survivor. Captain Stone, by his invaluable information and his subsequent sacrifice with the rearguard, saved the situation at the cost of his life. Lieut. Bezencry was seen to be wounded in the head. He continued to fight until he was killed.'

The report goes on to tell of huge masses of Germans mown down, heroic sacrifices, and a line at nightfall 'practically intact'.

'On the left of the brigade, however, the enemy succeeded in penetrating the line at one point, thus isolating a company of the Regt., who were in a small salient on the canal. During the remainder of the day and following night, repeated efforts were made to regain touch with this company, but without success ... At 4 p.m. the isolated company ... realising the improbability of being extricated, held a council of war, at which the two surviving company officers (Lieut. J. D. Robinson and Lieut. E. L. Corps), the C.S.M. (A. H.

Edwards), and platoon sergeants (Phillips, Parsons, Fairbrass, Lodge, and Legge) ... unanimously determined to fight to the last and have no surrender. Two runners who were sent to notify battalion headquarters of this succeeded in getting through, and this was the last known of this most gallant company.'

That was an Essex battalion at Moeuvres. One might say it was finer than Thermopylae; but it would be a desecration to cover the deed with a blanket of pompous words. It happened that the men of the A.I.F. were never confronted with a situation like this, and one dare not affirm that they would have done the same, however sure of it in our hearts we may be. Nevertheless, Fleurbaix indicated the lengths of unquestioning devotion to which they would go.

But the special excellence of the Australian soldier lay not so much in his valour, dash, adaptability and endurance, as in his mental resources — resources not solely confined to the hundreds of men of trained intellects in the ranks. There are thousands of instances. A private left alone in the desert with five hundred mutinous Arab workmen, had the duty (unusual, to say the least, for one of his rank) of building a railway. It was important work, for the Turks were striking at our communications, and were in fact within two or three miles of him. It had to be built at more than contract speed. After quelling a riot with the aid of half-a-dozen Tommies, he completed the line in two-thirds of the stipulated time.

Another private, during a critical stage of the German breakthrough on the Somme, took charge of a company (not of Australians), and having organised it to form a line, and having given its commander some candid but acute advice on the position, he reported back to his humble duties in his platoon. For the average Australian possesses a matured intellect which is capable of grappling with practically any emergency that may arise. It is an established fact that at least half the rank and file were capable of holding commissions with credit.

By appealing to his intelligence, one may exact discipline and respect for authority. But it is almost impossible to hoodwink him, for long before the matter has been officially presented to him, he will have had wind of it and formed his own conclusions. He is generally open to conviction; but convince him one must, or he will find some means, which will prove very difficult to counter, of evading the order.

*

One of the periodical outbursts of certain people who seemed to feel that they had to do something to justify their 'full-back' positions took the form of a frenzy of interrogation in regard to self-inflicted wounds. Men who had been hit in the line were subjected to humiliating questionings, and long report forms were sent to battalions to be filled in. Their mates were repeatedly bored by being asked on parade to supply information about the cases. One officer asked his company if anyone knew anything of the circumstances under which Private Blank became afflicted with shellshock. There was an oppressive silence, then a weary voice in the rear rank, 'Yair. Seen 'im drink some water out of a shell 'ole.'

On a quiet sector where a single man could easily give any necessary alarm in ample time, there was an order, more honoured in the breach than the observance, that no one should remove his equipment, night or day, and that every man should stand to arms at the appointed hours — a very vexatious and apparently needless precaution at that time. The company commander, being new to active service, insisted on its performance, and used to go around the trench to see it fulfilled. He was followed by a retainer. As he passed, the men threw grenades over the parapet, and as each one burst, the batman tapped the rim of his steel helmet. Ding! 'Another narrow escape, sir!' It was never long before the officer retired to his dugout 'to write my reports', and the men retired to theirs to sleep.

★

For several nights our passwords had been the names of racehorses. One night it was 'Revenue', a well-known cup-winner. A corporal who was a racing enthusiast, and who could give the pedigree of every famous horse for twenty years, was sent to a listening post with two men. A shell burst in the post, killing both men, and blowing the corporal almost to a sally port in the breastwork. Scrambling to his feet, he rushed in. 'Password!' hissed the sentry. 'Revenue,' gasped the other. 'Out of Shell-hole by High Explosive.'

★

169

At Fleurbaix, the whole of no man's land could be observed from our support and reserve lines, on the side of a hill. Whenever the German trench was 'strafed' with 'flying pigs' (the old heavy trench mortars), the garrison were withdrawn from the front line. As the 'pigs' thundered on the enemy trench, our parapets in supports and reserves were dotted with a black row of heads, in a double line of half a mile. Then up would go the cry 'Two duckboards and a Fritz', and up would go all the hats, as our men applauded like spectators at a football match.

They had quaint tastes in marching songs. For example, how often has one seen a battalion of men on the road, up to the ankles in slush, singing at the top of their voices these words to the tune of 'A Wee Deoch and Doris', merrily pounding past one kilometre stone after another while the Colonel so pointedly referred to rode sedately at the head of the battalion!

'Good bye Major —,
And Colonel —, too,
Ever since we left Australia
We've been messed around by you.
Gallipoli was a failure,
And Pozières a farce;
Take your rotten old A.I.F. to Hell,
For I've got my Blighty pass.'

And they did not mean a single word of it. Or again —

'I'm a rag-time soldier, a dopey, ragged, ragtime soldier,
Out on parade every morning,
Standing at the corner with me rifle on me shoulder,
A rag-time soldier,

Happy as the birds in May,
Fighting for me King and me country,
On a lousy dollar a day.'
Another of the same tenor ('Looking This Way'): —
'Bill Birdwood's Army!
Five bob a day!
If you should grumble
The Colonel will say,
'Put him in the guard tent
And stop his pay.'
Oh, what an Army!
Five bob a day.'

One may deplore their lack of respect for venerable things, as when they called the Virgin and Child hanging head downwards from the top of Albert's ruined basilica by the nickname of Fanny Durack, the Champion Lady Diver, and dubbed the streets of Péronne 'Dingbat Alley' or 'Roo de Kanga', but their amazing selfconfidence, their intense clannishness and their fervent patriotism atoned for all defects.

They had a wonderful capacity for adapting themselves to circumstances. Being billeted in a Frenchman's cowshed, it was rarely that they did not succeed in ingratiating themselves with the family, and in taking up quarters within the house. So also, it was always an object lesson in homemaking to see a battalion of men arrive on a barren, muddy hill where there was no apparent vestige of building material. No matter how weary, every man within an hour would have a more or less comfortable dugout, roofed with planking, galvanised iron, or old garments taken to pieces and sewn in the form of a tent.

A platoon was as near to the socialist ideal as it was possible to be. Certainly money had not the value it did in civil life, because one never knew if one would live to enjoy it. 'Eat, drink and be merry as possible, for tomorrow we may get knocked,' was the prevailing faith. And therefore gambling had a wide appeal, for the sordid aspect was largely lacking. They gambled anywhere, in the Line or in Trafalgar Square while the police strike was on — at the time when the Australians, with rather a patronising desire to assist the population, voluntarily and quite efficiently regulated the traffic of London.

Most men had an acute business sense. Many invested their winnings in struggling French businesses, and saw their money increased every time they came down from the Line.

They were extraordinary people: tenacious but loveable. Everyone knows their quality in battle. But it should be borne in mind that the vast majority of Australian battles were fought by men who had gone hungry and sleepless for days; that many of the men were convalescents taken before their time from hospitals, owing to the shortage of reinforcements; and that all were weary, debilitated in body and weakened in nerve by long months — or years — under a strain such as no considerable numbers of men have ever before been called upon to endure.

American infantry took over the Australian trenches on 25 September 1918—the first day since 7 April 1916 that Australians had not manned some part of the Western Front. On 29 September the Americans attacked the Hindenburg Line at Bellicourt. They made good progress but neglected to mop up, and the Australians following, including Downing's 57th Battalion, had to fight hard to clear the ground.

XIX

BELLICOURT
29th September to 2nd October, 1918

Owing to the tragic weakness of all our battalions, two American divisions of a total strength in infantry of about thirty-three thousand were attached to the Australian Corps. They were the 27th and 30th Divisions. One had had a single tour of duty in the line in a quiet sector, the other had never been in action.

Preliminary attacks were made by the 1st and 4th Divisions, which advanced the line beyond Hargicourt, to within hitting distance of the Hindenburg system. We marched from Péronne to a ravine at Hargicourt, beside a huge mound, ringed around by platforms in rising concentric tiers, where once the enemy had placed guns to fire down into our distant trenches. It was honeycombed with tunnels.

The Yanks were in the dugouts.

'Any room, America?'

'Come right in. Guess we're glad we're havin' you boys with us in the shootin' gall'ry.'

We crawled in, and lay and listened to the queer roll

of their voices and drowsed, for we had marched long and far. Shells were falling here and there. One fell on a gun belonging to a battery in the ravine. There were cries of 'Stretcher-bearers, stretcher-bearers!'

Next day we occupied ourselves with the issuing of the impedimenta of battle. American officers were standing among groups of their sergeants, vehemently explaining the orders. Their men were playing games, ignorant that they would need all the sleep they could get, that this was probably the last chance for days.

The two strong American divisions were to take the first objective — the main Hindenburg Line — assisted by a tremendous British barrage, and a huge fleet of British tanks. They were to be followed by the 3rd and 5th Australian Divisions, which together scarcely totalled ten thousand infantry, and which were detailed to take the second and third objectives, the Le Catelet and Beaurevoir Lines.

Long before dawn on the twenty-ninth of September there were loud voices in the mist, and we heard the Yanks being roused to battle. There were the noises of preparation, then a silence, a curt nasal order, and they were gone.

A brief and troubled sleep, and we heard the barrage open. We crawled out of our shelters and mounted a bank to watch. The ground was quivering with the recoil of thousands of guns. The din was ear-splitting. One could not hear one's own voice. The line where the guns were was like a rift in the earth's crust, through which volcanic flames were shooting upwards. Big guns were slamming and booming on every side. A mile ahead, the eighteen-pounder batteries were heard in a continuous baritone chuckle. In front we could see nothing but a cloud of smoke over the battle. Enemy shells were bursting all around, but we could distinguish neither their scream nor their crash. This is why one fears a thousand shells in battle far less than a single shell behind the lines. The shelling grew hotter, so we went to the illusory refuge of the ravine.

When we fell in, dawn had broken. We made our way, in small parties at intervals, to a quarry where there was a dressing station. A few American wounded had already come in. We trudged along hedges, over shell-torn roads, across hills and through valleys, till we came to a trench. It was dug and reinforced on the English plan. It was obviously the trench where the initial fury of the German attack had fallen in March.

We wound through. In places it was blown in, elsewhere blocked by twisted wire and galvanised iron. Then we went across the open, over what had been no man's land that morning. We heard American wounded crying out. We found a few and bandaged their wounds. The morning mist and the smoke from our phosphorous shells had mingled in an impenetrable blanket of fog. A shell fell among half a dozen of our men, and up they went in the air, and down they came with the clods of dirt, as smoking bundles of bloody rags.

We followed the levelled paths of tanks through forests of barbed wire, then came to a deep canyon of a trench whose sides were built of concrete — twelve feet deep and twelve feet wide. There were deep dugouts at intervals. It was the first trench of the Hindenburg Line, the main bulwark of the Fatherland.

Thence through the smoke to the daylight —

through net-spread thickets of wire for a mile, and across successive belts of trenches to a hill which was bare except for one brown stripe of wire athwart its green bosom. Suddenly a machine-gun rattled, then another and another. Several men dropped, writhing. We took cover in shellholes. All the troops to the right and left had done the same. A breath of wind blew away the thinning strands of smoke and let in a brief gleam of sunlight. We advanced warily from cover to cover. Men dropped in their tracks, a few for every hundred yards.

We could not at first understand it. The Americans had gone forward, yet now there was no sign of them. They had not come back. They had not been wiped out, for we had not seen any bodies. They seemed to have had an easy passage, so why were the enemy here? The bullets were coming from left and right, but not from in front. We advanced by sectional rushes, a few dashing forward at a time, while the remainder gave covering fire, but we could see nothing to fire at. We heard a flurry of fire from our Lewis guns on the left, then our neighbours began running forward by twos and threes. Some of them got into one end of a trench. We saw and heard bombing. Then the remainder of them dashed forward. There seemed to be some kind of a scuffle, then our men passed over the place. We could not see what they had done to the Germans. We could guess. Much the same was happening far on the right.

We ourselves encountered no German posts, but one of our battalions was much less fortunate. Two of its companies, finding no one at the place where they expected to 'leap-frog' the Americans, went on, thinking the latter to be a little farther ahead. The quietness

178

encouraged them in this opinion. Then machine-guns opened on every side. They had walked into a trap. The Germans had waited until they were inside, and had closed the exit. But they found that entrapping Australians was like shutting their hand on a thistle. Nevertheless, by the time our men had cut their way out, they had lost two-thirds of their number; and this was before their part in the battle had begun.

At length, pushing through the desultory fire, we entered Bellicourt. It was full of Americans. What had occurred was now apparent. Following the custom of most troops with more spirit than experience, they had gone as far as their feet would take them, and in their impetuous haste had neglected either to throw bombs down the dugouts or to capture their occupants. Consequently, the enemy came out of the earth and cut them off.

We lined the mound above the tunnel through which ran the Canal du Nord. *Crash!* One of the men spun high in the air and fell awry. His face was turned to his back. He looked as though a giant had twisted him in his hands as one would wring a damp cloth. The shelling grew heavier.

We were to go forward at midday, but the plans had gone wrong. We were to have had a barrage with us, but there were known to be numerous parties of Americans in front — some, in fact, were three miles further on — although what had become of them was hard to say. As a result, our artillery could not fire. We were given the help of tanks instead. We were by now reduced to about half our strength.

About four o'clock in the afternoon we advanced

from the mound, in artillery formation. Except for a fair number of shells, we did not come under fire until we reached a sunken road on the top of a hill some four hundred yards in front of the canal. There the enemy laid down his barrage. The tanks, excepting only two or three, were hit and put out of action one by one, as they tried to climb the steep side of the cutting. Several burst into flames. Thereafter, we kept as far away from the tanks as we possibly could. They drew too many shells. We were now moving to the right, almost parallel to the general conformation of our line. We hurried through the region of the hottest shelling, and walked down the forward slopes of the hill. We found ourselves out of the frying pan and in the fire. Machine-guns were chattering on the left. The air was thick with bullets. Our boys were falling like apples from branches in a gale. The clothing and equipment of each man of the remainder had at least one bullet hole in them. We could now see the German batteries shooting from some mounds not two thousand yards away. At the foot of our hill was a railway embankment. The remaining tanks and infantry sheltered for some time behind it, relatively safe for a time.

The few remaining tanks were unable to find a way over the high, perpendicular sides of the sunken road, so thereafter we went on alone. We dashed across the railway in twos and threes, but the machine-guns on the left were waiting for us every time a man moved. A further number were hit by the skimming bullets, but most of us got over. We occupied a trench on the other side, which ran directly to the village of Nauroy, immediately in front and almost at a right angle to the embankment. We lined the trench and opened fire on the enemy. We were now facing left (compared with the direction in which we had advanced), for the enemy was firing from the Le Catelet line, which at that point formed a salient into the Australian position. We were at the apex of a triangle, of which each side was about one thousand yards long. The railway was the left leg, the trench running to Nauroy was the right leg, and that portion of the Le Catelet line between Nauroy and the railway was the base.

While this was happening, the men of the 8th Brigade had pushed sideways from the right into Nauroy. They now began bombing along the Le Catelet line from the village. At the same time we climbed out of our trench and advanced across the open. We were not, however, met by the same withering fire as before, thanks to the diversion caused by the Eighth. As we entered the German trench, the enemy bombed and shot at us for a little, then retired to its continuation on the left of the railway line. He contented himself with throwing a few bombs over the embankment, which was low at this point. We returned them with interest.

An hour later, reinforced by a company, we crossed the railway, driving the enemy before us. He fought hard at first; then, seeing that we were not to be denied, he retreated to a maze of trenches around Cabaret Farm. We gathered ourselves to attack this stronghold. We bombed the enemy out of several trenches but we were held up by machine-guns and uncut wire, always an insuperable combination of difficulties.

That night and for the next two days we held the line, for the situation had not been made clear on our flanks. There were bomb fights and attempts to drive the enemy out of Cabaret Farm. There was almost continuous fighting, but of a desultory nature; and the Germans still held their strong post.

Since leaving Bellicourt, we had several times gone over parties of isolated Americans in shellholes, who seemed pleased to see us. They had reason. We attached them as a very welcome reinforcement to our weak platoons, which had been at first about thirty strong. They now consisted of six or seven men. The American divisions were relieved that night.

We were now waiting for the chance to attack anew. We returned the Americans to their units, and held the line while the enemy shelled. The effect of shellfire is cumulative. To each shell is added the moral effect of all that have preceded it. One's first shell is a contemptible circumstance. One's ten-thousandth is a tragedy, even if it misses.

On the morning of 1st October we received, without warning, orders to advance. At dawn a barrage of smoke-shells fell in an exact line before our feet, and we went forward in two lines of skirmishers. We had one glimpse of the German artillery being pulled away by horses, and then the smoke hid everything. Cabaret Farm, around which there had been so many little fights in the past sixty hours, gave little trouble. The Germans, after firing their machine-guns, surrendered readily. We drove them from the first trench of the Beaurevoir system. Then we advanced to a farm near Estrees. The Huns were very much surprised to see us, and again we made easy progress. But on sweeping over the summit of a ridge, we came into view of the main German position, to which he had retired; and for the third time in three days we were caught in the German barrage, for the third time caught in unsubdued machine-gun fire. By now there were so few of us left that a further advance was out of the question. We dug in.

At two o'clock next morning we were relieved by the 2nd Division, about to push forward to the storming of Montbrehain. We were never to see the line again.

The 2nd Division's capture of Montbrehain broke the Beaurevoir Line, the last great German defensive system in the West. The Division was then withdrawn, the last Australians to quit the Western Front. In November the A.I.F. prepared to return. The Germans surrendered first.

EPILOGUE

'To you who have known so much good and so much evil in the years that have gone in flames, these lines are given.

For you every grief will be ennobled by the memory of the generous and the spacious and the terrible things which you have confronted as things befitting your own great souls, without regrets, while the mill-stones of Fate were grinding out the future so doubtfully, so very, very slowly.'

There is first the pleasure of lying in the sun on a quiet day, in a quiet sector. Next there is the joy of leaving the Line on such a day, with a mission in a town. This was rare. The memory stands forth largely of the way the soul exulted after days on the rack had passed, when we came from the Line. Neither does one forget the lesser relief of 'Stand down', when daylight comes in those evil places, to those worn with watching through the interminable night, and through that last hour before

185

dawn when the soul is ridden by chimeras, and body and mind are oppressed by a horrible weariness.

There is also the fresh, tingling air of early morning in autumn, as when you and I, my friend, walked from Brucamps, in 1916, the day before we went forward to the Somme. We mounted a long hill and entered the dark shade of huge elms where there was a village on a road which wandered aimlessly under the trees to a white-washed *estaminet* with green shutters, and emerged on the brow of a steep hill. Below us, on a little plain, the armies of France passed by. Their long blue columns stretched from a hilltop in the north to the southern horizon. The hems of their greatcoats were buttoned behind them, leaving the legs free, their helmets were like the morions of their ancestors.

The columns passed near us like a river of armed men. They were full of the cheerfulness of schoolboys, a traditional quality of the French infantry. They laughed to each other and waved to us.

There were those bright mornings in January when I walked with you, my friend, before you were killed at Proyart. We went over the high snow-covered hills from Sequieres to Doudeauville in Pas-de-Calais. Do you remember?

There were dreamy afternoons at Steenbecque, at harvest time; and Zoe, rare and bright and innocent, and funny little old 'Madame Fini', who was four feet high and put her head between her knees to laugh; and Marie and Yvonne in sailor blouses at the *estaminet*, where one was very welcome, and always of the family. There we spent pleasant evenings until the gendarmes intimated that it was eight o'clock, and closing time. Then we would return to a room we had hired in a cottage where the creepers grew, down a lane; and we smoked and played cards and sang to the ceiling.

There were nights of revelry on the Somme, after we came out from Zenith Trench to 'E' Camp, or from Monsoon to Delville Wood, among the batteries of nine-point-twos; when the rum came, and sometimes a bottle of whisky, and tinned fruit and lobster, procured from the canteen at Bernafay Siding on the Decauville railway. There was the night when the lance-corporal of the Jocks, a liar of purest ray serene and a humourist of whom the memory still refreshes me, awoke the adjutant by chanting sagas to the tingling stars; and that worthy stood outside our dugout in the frozen trench, and cursed us all (but we heeded him not) till the Scot returned to his uncongenial associates on the bleak hill of High Wood, weeping for what grief or sin I know not.

It is now a heavy thing to speak of that night in the huts at Fricourt, in February, when long Mac solemnly executed a sword dance with the Regimental Sergeant Major; and Richard, the well-beloved, woke the camp warden for a song; and an area commandant was sent home glorious in his wonder at the 'extrorn' Antipodeans'; and of the time when someone (dare I say who?) solemnly rowed himself to his bunk in a soap-box believing himself to be torpedoed at sea; or of when we came on a company commander at midnight in the empty square of Huppy offering nails to drive into a figure claimed to be Hindenburg, for 'deux sous a go, in aid of the Ludendorff Loan'. So we brought him home with us, and we took a major's gate off its hinges for its resemblance to a harp, and we serenaded him till the provost sergeant came foaming.

There were long summer afternoons in the Bois de Mai, near Cardonette and Allonville, where the race meeting was held. There were uproarious functions in the messes; but the boon companions dropped off one by one — and sad was the meagre crowd that sat round tables that never seemed so large and empty as after a heavy 'stunt'.

Lastly there were rich and sacramental things — the love of comrades, letters from home, the present comradeship of those gone West, whom we do not at all times regret, for they still guide us, in whose arms they died,

> 'The goodliest fellowship of famous knights
> Whereof this world holds record. Such a sleep
> They sleep — the men I loved.'

Especially there was one killed on his way to the line. We passed him as we hurried from one sector to another during the fight. He was sitting as was his wont in life, with his head in his hands, and his elbows on his knees, on the lip of a shellhole; so we bade him farewell and passed.

At sunset when 'Retreat' is blown, we rise and watch the sun go down, thinking on the soldier souls that travel with it, sinking at evening in the west, rising in the morning in a daily resurrection. That is a comforting thing.

For the lively day after the weariness of night, sunshine after greyness, journey's end, rest after labour, and

188

the endowment of liberty, I give thanks to the friendly
Genii of earth.

THE END

Appendix

ROLL OF HONOUR
57th Battalion Killed 1916 — 1918

AK - Accidentally Killed
DAD - Died after Discharge
DOD - Died of Disease

DOS - Died of Sickness (abroad)
DOSA - Died of Sickness (Aust)
DOW - Died of Wound s(France)

DOWA - Died of Wounds (Aust)
KIA - Killed in Action
NK - Not Known

OFFICERS

Aram, Capt J.T. H.	25.9.17	KIA
Dickinson, Capt H.S.	25.9.17	KIA
Harris, Capt F.W.	20.8.16	KIA
Morgan, Capt R.A.	25.4.18	DOW
Allen, Lieut W.R.	1.2.17	KIA
Anderson, Lieut E.H.	15.12.16	KIA
Bartlett, Lieut A.T.	17.9.19	DOS
Davis, Lieut A.	27.2.19	DOS
Falconer, Lieut J.A.	25.4.18	KIA
Gowenlock, Lieut E.S.	10.4.18	DOW
Hedgecock, Lieut A.H.	31.8.18	DOW
Joynt, Lieut G.V.W.	25.9.17	KIA
Kerr, Lieut R.J.L.	23.4.18	KIA
Marxsen, Lieut R.	3.9.18	KIA
Miller, Lieut A.H.	25.9.17	KIA
Muter, Lieut R.	25.4.18	KIA
Nicholson, Lieut P.F.	5.4.18	KIA
Snowball, Lieut J.I.	14.8.18	DOW
St. Pinnock, Lieut C.C.D.	20.8.16	KIA
Sutherland, Lieut E.B.	22.9.16	KIA
Thomson, Lieut J.J.	29.9.18	DOW

OTHER RANKS

Abrahamson, Pte A.	20.7.16	KIA
Adams, Pte F.C.	19.8.16	DOW
Agnew, Pte S.W.	26.9.17	KIA
Alphey, Pte A.R.	25.9.17	KIA
Anglin, Pte M.	20.7.16	KIA
Arbon, Pte R.E.	19.7.16	DOW
Archer, Pte A.	27.2.18	KIA
Arthur, Pte D.W.	18.2.19	DOS
Ashford, Pte H.G.	23.11.16	KIA
Ashley, Pte T.F.	30.9.18	KIA

Baker, Pte R.J.	28.9.18	KIA
Baker, Pte V.R.	15.10.17	KIA
Bannister, Pte L.C.	4.2.19	DOSA
Bastian, Pte R.C.	15.2.17	DOW
Baxter, Pte H.R.	15.7.16	KIA
Beath, Sgt R.	3.10.18	DOW
Bell, Pte D. McK.	28.10.16	KIA
Bell, Pte H.H.	28.10.16	KIA
Bell, Pte S.A.	8.8.18	KIA
Best, Pte F.T.	26.3.17	KIA
Beswick, Pte L.E.	26.9.17	KIA
Bibbs, Pte L.B.C.D.	28.4.18	KIA
Birrell, Pte R.	25.4.18	KIA
Bisset, Pte D.P.	19.9.18	KIA
Black, Pte M.R.	8.8.18	DOW
Bladen, Pte L.	12.3.18	DOW
Blandford, L-Cpl T.	9.5.17	KIA
Boothroyd, Pte H.H.	15.10.17	KIA
Bowring, Pte R.J.L. (also known as Bevan)	12.10.16	KIA
Boxall, Pte W.R.	11.7.16	KIA
Bradley, Pte R.D.	11.7.16	KIA
Bradshaw, Pte W.H.	1.10.18	KIA
Bray, Pte E.L.	4.7.18	KIA
Breustedt, Pte L.L.	25.9.17	KIA
Brierley, Cpl A.	26.9.17	KIA
Bright, Pte S.W.	20.3.17	KIA
Brinsmead, Pte A.J.	22.11.16	KIA
Bristow, Pte C.	27.9.17	KIA
Brogmus, Pte D.	29.9.18	KIA
Brook, Pte W.	9.8.16	KIA
Brooks, Pte R.J.	25.9.17	KIA
Brown, Pte W.A.	29.9.18	KIA
Brown, Pte W.E.	2.8.16	DOW
Brown, Pte W.E.C.	7.12.16	DOD
Bryant, Pte G.F.	14.2.17	DOD

Buchan, Pte W.F.	21.7.16	KIA	Daly, Pte J.	27.9.17	KIA
Bull, Sgt W.W.	20.7.16	KIA	(also known as Hart, J)		
Buller, Sgt A.A.	11.5.17	DOW	Daniell, Pte J.M.	15.7.16	KIA
Buller, Pte C.E.	19.9.17	DOW	Dann, Pte L.W.	16.7.17	DOW
Burgess, Pte E.H.	16.10.17	KIA	Dargatz, Pte N.F.	26.4.18	DOW
Burley, Pte E.L.	10.8.18	DOW	Dark, Pte A.C.	29.8.18	KIA
Byrne, Pte C.F.	25.4.18	DOW	Darrelle, Sgt R.T.	22.4.18	DOW
Caddle, L-Sgt W.J.	19.2.17	DOW	Davey, Pte E.C.	25.2.18	KIA
Cahill, Pte J.J.	16.3.17	DOS	Davey, L-Sgt J.F.	26.4.18	KIA
Campbell, Pte C.G.	11.3.18	KIA	Davies, Pte D.	25.9.17	KIA
Campbell, Pte E.C.	6.2.19	DOS	Davies, Pte G.F.	25.10.17	KIA
Campbell, Pte R.W.	23.11.16	KIA	Davies, Sgt H.M.	22.7.16	DOW
Campbell, Pte T.	29.9.18	KIA	Davis, Pte A.H.	29.9.18	DOW
Campbell, Pte W.C.	26.9.17	KIA	Davis, Pte T.	25.9.17	KIA
Cann, Pte G.L.	29.9.18	KIA	Dean, Pte L.	4.7.18	KIA
Carter, Pte A.B.	29.9.18	KIA	Delahey, Pte W.J.	5.4.18	KIA
Carroll, Pte J.	20.4.19	DOSUK	Devitt, Pte P.J.	1.10.18	KIA
Cawse, Cpl F.W.	26.9.17	KIA	Dodemaide, Pte F.J.	24.3.17	KIA
Chapman, Pte A.E.	2.9.17	AK	Dodgson, Pte W.	30.9.18	KIA
Chapman, Pte F.	25.9.17	KIA	Dooley, Pte A.J.	13.5.17	KIA
Christie, Pte R.	23.5.18	DOW	Doran, Pte H.P.	26.9.17	KIA
Clarke, Pte A.R.	25.9.17	KIA	Dowsey, Pte I.	11.7.16	KIA
Clayton, Pte A.N.	21.8.16	DOW	Drew, Pte J.	5.4.18	DOW
Cleary, Pte W.C.	15.3.17	KIA	Dudley, Pte T.E.	25.2.18	KIA
Clinton, Pte R.G.	22.11.16	KIA	Duncombe, Pte E.S.	25.9.17	KIA
Coad, Pte C.	19.8.16	KIA	Dunn, Pte T.D.	12.9.18	DOS
Cock, Pte J.A.	25.4.18	KIA	Dutfield, Pte A.	5.3.18	KIA
Collie, Pte G.G.	20.1.17	KIA	Eddy, Sgt E.E.	31.7.19	DOWA
Colling, Sgt C.	30.9.18	KIA	Eddy, L-Cpl G.	2.4.17	KIA
Collins, Pte L.M.N.W.	5.10.18	DOW	Edwards, Pte C.P.	27.9.17	DOW
(also known as West-Collins)			Edwards, Pte J.W.	26.9.17	KIA
Connell, Pte J.B.	27.9.17	KIA	Edwards, Pte P.A.	8.8.18	KIA
Conway, Pte F.W.	12.5.17	KIA	Edwards, Pte W.G.	15.7.16	KIA
Conway, Pte J.P.	12.5.17	KIA	Egan, Cpl M.J.	11.3.18	KIA
Cook, Pte F.W.	19.8.16	KIA	Eldershaw, Pte A.G.	20.7.16	KIA
Cook, Pte P.	13.3.17	KIA	Ellens, Pte A.H.	29.9.18	KIA
Cook, Pte P.H.	17.9.17	KIA	Elston, Pte A.H.	26.2.17	KIA
Cook, Pte W.J.	26.9.17	KIA	Emmett, Pte R.	30.8.18	KIA
Corrigan, L-Cpl W.H.	8.8.18	KIA	Evans, Pte S.	26.5.18	KIA
Cossar, Pte J.L.	12.5.17	KIA	Fagg, Pte W.	26.4.18	DOW
Cousins, Pte W.J.	9.2.17	DOW	Fahey, Pte M.S.	16.10.17	KIA
Crawford, Pte R.S.	19.8.16	KIA	Farnell, Pte A.E.	9.8.16	DOW
Cropley, Pte G.F.	26.9.17	KIA	Farrands, Sgt A.V.	8.8.18	KIA
Crozier, Pte F.	17.7.16	DOW	Faulkner, Pte C.E.T.	12.4.18	KIA
Cumming, Pte A.R.	27.9.17	KIA	Featherstone, Pte J.F.V.	21.3.18	KIA
Curnow, Pte T.	8.8.18	KIA	Felgenhauer, Cpl F.C.	29.9.18	KIA
Curry, Cpl R.A.	16.10.17	KIA	Fernance, Pte A.	20.7.16	KIA

Ferrari, Pte J.W.	20.7.16	KIA	Harvey, Pte W.J.	26.10.17	KIA
Ferrow, Pte C.W.	28.2.17	DOS	Haw, Pte M.B.	3.11.17	DOW
Fish, Pte A.	31.3.19	DOS	Hawker, L-Cpl A.	25.9.17	KIA
Flavell, Pte G.E.	26.3.17	KIA	Hazell, Pte A.	27.9.17	KIA
Fletcher, Pte J.D.	12.9.18	DODUK	Heard, Pte R.T.	21.3.18	KIA
Forsyth, L-Cpl E.J.	23.7.16	KIA	Heddell, Pte T.H.	25.9.17	KIA
Forsyth, Pte K.K.	16.10.17	DOW	Henderson, Pte L.	20.7.16	DOW
Fossey, Pte C.V.	25.11.16	DOW	Henson, Pte G.L.	28.9.18	DOW
Fraser, Pte J.F.	13.5.17	KIA	Hickin, Pte J.	27.7.17	DOS
Fraser, Pte J.W.	9.9.16	DOW	Hicks, Pte C.H.	12.5.17	KIA
Freeman, Pte H.	23.11.16	DPOW	Hill, Pte D.	3.4.17	DOD
Fregon, Pte F.	25.3.17	DOW	Hinchliffe, Pte T.W.	22.11.16	DOW
Fregon, Pte R.A.	23.11.16	KIA	Hocking, Pte W.F.	5.4.18	KIA
Frost, Pte G.	26.9.17	KIA	Hodgetts, Pte C.J.	29.9.18	KIA
Fuller, Pte C.L.	1.10.18	KIA	Hodgkison, Pte J.	26.9.17	KIA
Fyfe, L-Cpl W.B.	8.8.18	KIA	Hogan, Cpl A.H.	18.7.16	DOW
Gallin, Pte F.	25.9.18	KIA	Hogg, Pte B.M.	12.5.17	DOW
Garden, Pte G.S.	16.8.18	DOW	Hogg, Pte J.A.	12.5.17	DOW
Gleeson, Pte C.J.J.	3.5.18	DOW	Holland, Cpl E.M.	1.10.18	KIA
Godden, Pte F.E.	28.11.16	KIA	Holmes, Cpl G.T.	26.3.17	KIA
Graham, Pte G.	28.9.17	DOW	Homer, Cpl A.H.	7.7.18	DOW
Graham, Cpl W.H.	11.3.18	KIA	Homer, Cpl V.W.M.	27.2.18	KIA
Grandfield, Pte G.A.	25.9.17	KIA	Hood, Pte J.A.	12.5.17	KIA
Grant, Pte S.W.	20.7.16	KIA	Hood, Pte L.G.	26.5.18	KIA
Grass, Pte L. McK.	27.9.17	KIA	Houston, Cpl F.G.	8.12.16	DOS
Green, Pte J.	25.4.18	KIA	Howard, Pte H.S.J.	21.3.18	DOW
Gregory, Pte J.M.	5.4.18	DOD	Howard, Sgt R.S.	22.5.18	DOW
Gregory, Pte W.	19.7.16	KIA	Howlett, Pte J.B.	16.10.18	DOW
Gregory, Pte W.H.	27.11.16	DOS	Hughes, Pte M.J.	25.9.17	KIA
Guilmartin, Pte G.H.	25.9.17	KIA	Hughes, Pte S.R.	5.3.18	DOW
Hales, Pte W.J.	25.4.18	DOW	Hume, Pte W.	9.3.17	DOW
Hall, Pte H.A.T.	21.12.16	KIA	Hummerston, Pte G.	26.4.18	DOW
Hall, Pte S.F.	14.5.17	DOW	Hunt, Pte A.	8.8.18	KIA
Hallberg, Pte J.H.W.	4.3.18	KIA	Hunter, Sgt R.J.	15.11.17	DOW
Hallett, Sgt R.R.	31.7.16	KIA	Imrie, Pte E.A.	27.10.17	KIA
Hamber, Pte J.	1.9.18	KIA	Inglefinger, Pte L.C.	27.8.16	KIA
Hamilton, Pte W.H.	27.8.16	KIA	Ingleton, Pte C.H.	24.7.16	DOW
Hammond, Pte F.E.	26.9.17	KIA	Ingram, Pte J.	1.12.16	DOW
Hancock, Pte A.J.	14.10.17	KIA	Ireland, Pte V.	15.8.16	KIA
Hanger, A/Cpl A.J.	25.3.17	DOW	Jacks, Pte L.T.	12.4.18	DOW
Hannasky, Pte F.M.	24.11.16	KIA	Jackson, L-Cpl H.E.	2.10.18	DOW
Hardingham, Pte C.	11.7.16	KIA	Jacobson, Pte H.W.	26.3.17	DOW
Hardwick, Pte S.F.	12.5.17	KIA	Jacobson, Pte J.	22.11.16	DOWA
Harris, Pte G.L.	5.3.18	KIA	Jarman, Sgt W.	4.7.18	KIA
Harris, Pte J.S.	26.9.17	KIA	Jason, L-Cpl C.V.	13.8.19	KIA
Harvey, Cpl R.A.	12.12.16	KIA	Jenkin, Pte G.E.	19.7.16	KIA
Harvey, Pte V.D.C.	1.10.18	DOW	Jessup, Sgt A.E.	13.8.16	DOW

Name	Date		Name	Date	
Johnson, Pte H.	26.4.18	KIA	Malcolm, Pte W.	25.2.18	KIA
Johnston, Pte A.H.M.	29.9.18	KIA	Malone, Pte J.H.	26.9.17	KIA
Jolliffe, Pte F.	29.9.18	KIA	Manallack, Pte W.	26.9.17	KIA
Jones, Pte C.M.	10.12.16	DOW	Mancer, Pte F.C,	12.12.17	KIA
Jones, Pte E.S.	4.2.19	DOS	Mann, Sgt T.H.	24.3.17	KIA
Jones, L–Cpl W.T.	13.5.17	KIA	Margules, Pte T.R.	27.10.17	DOW
Jurey, Pte F.L.	20.7.16	DOS	Mark, Pte F.	26.9.17	KIA
Keane, Pte J.G.	9.3.17	KIA	Marshall, Pte G.H.S.	27.9.17	KIA
Kee, Pte J.E.	26.9.17	KIA	Martin, Pte G.E.	28.10.17	DOW
Kelleher, Pte T.	25.10.17	KIA	Martin, Pte T.E.	27.3.17	DOW
Kennewell, Pte C.J.	22.11.18	DOS	Martin, Pte W.E.	17.10.17	KIA
Kenny, Pte J.F.	17.7.16	DOW	Martin, Pte W.W.	26.9.17	KIA
Kerr, Pte A.	5.10.18	DOW	Martinelli, Pte H.B.	25.2.18	KIA
Kerr, Sgt A.	20.7.16	KIA	Maybury, L–Cpl S.C.	8.8.18	KIA
Kerr, Pte J.	5.4.18	DOW	McAdam, Pte G.S.	3.9.18	KIA
King, Pte A.W.	12.5.17	KIA	McAuley, Pte E.G.	2.3.18	KIA
King, Pte D.F.	25.9.17	KIA	McCahery, Pte P.J.	26.4.18	KIA
King, Pte L.V.	15.7.16	KIA	McCart, Pte C.	25.10.17	KIA
King, Sgt W.J.	25.2.18	KIA	McConnell, L–Cpl W.J.	2.4.17	KIA
Kinsey, Pte F.A.	23.3.18	DOW	McConnell, Pte W.J.N.	22.7.16	DOW
Kirby, Pte W.	2.4.17	DOW	McCoppin, Pte J.R.	26.9.17	KIA
Knight, Pte R.O.	25.2.18	KIA	McCracken, Pte J.N.	27.9.17	KIA
Kuhne, Pte A.G.	25.9.17	KIA	McDonald, Pte A.	26.9.17	KIA
Ladson, Pte W.S.	16.10.18	DOW	McDonald, Pte D.	15.7.16	KIA
Lain, Pte J.	7.9.18	DOW	McDonald, Pte H.L.	27.9.17	KIA
Lambert, Pte A.	4.9.18	KIA	McDonald, Pte H.U.	15.5.17	DOW
Latta, Pte W.T.	26.4.18	KIA	McGain, Pte R.J.	30.8.18	KIA
Leed, Pte D.R.	15.7.16	KIA	McGeary, Pte J.	12.11.17	DAD
Le Tisser, Pte A.	19.12.16	DOS	McGrath, Pte P.	15.3.17	KIA
Lester, Pte H.C.	26.9.17	KIA	McGregor, Pte C.L.	29.1.17	DOW
Lever, Pte S.E.	24.9.17	KIA	McGregor, Sgt J.	24.3.17	KIA
Lewis, Pte G.H.	9.4.18	KIA	McIntyre, Pte D.S.	9.11.16	DOW
Lindley, Pte W.	21.9.17	KIA	McKay, Pte W.	27.9.17	KIA
Livick, Pte J.	12.12.17	KIA	McKee, Dvr H.	3.10.18	DOW
Locke, Cpl W.R.	19.8.16	KIA	McMahon, Pte J.	25.4.18	KIA
Lockyer, Pte N.A.	25.9.17	KIA	McPhee, Pte S.C.	8.8.18	KIA
Lucas, Pte P.C.	9.12.18	DOS	Metelmann, Pte C.J.	26.8.17	KIA
Lugg, Pte N.W.H.	26.10.17	KIA	Milgate, Pte S.V.	16.10.17	KIA
Lugton, Pte J.A.	9.8.18	DOW	Mills, Pte E.G.	27.10.17	KIA
Luke, Pte W.H.	27.4.18	DOW	Mitchell, Pte F.W.	11.8.18	DOW
Lynch, Pte E.	27.2.18	KIA	Mitchell, Pte J.L.R.	16.10.17	KIA
Lyon, Sgt J.S.	23.2.19	DOS	Mitchell, L–Cpl W.J.	13.2.17	KIA
Macbryde, Pte G.A.	17.8.18	DOW	Mitchell, Pte W.W.	3.12.16	DOW
Mackay, Pte A.	19.8.16	KIA	Montgomery, Pte A.L.	25.9.16	KIA
Macklin, Pte J.F.	11.3.18	KIA	Moore, Pte L.W.	26.4.18	DOW
Mahony, Pte M.F.	21.5.17	DOW	Morris, Pte G.J.T.	15.4.18	KIA
Makepeace, Pte P.A.G.	24.9.17	KIA	Morrison, Pte H.H.	27.7.16	DOW

Morrow, Cpl S.	18.8.18	KIA	Rees, Pte W.	14.10.17	KIA
Moulton, Sgt L.L.	26.7.16	DOW	Reis, L–Cpl H.J.	14.5.17	DOW
Muir, Pte I.C.	26.10.17	DOW	Richards, Pte D.G.	23.6.17	DOSUK
Mullard, Pte E.C.	11.8.18	DOW	Riddell, Pte A.H.T.	13.8.18	DOW
Mullins, Pte A.J.	27.7.16	KIA	Ridding, Pte T.	22.9.16	KIA
Mulquinney, Pte J.J.	26.4.18	KIA	Roberts, Pte O.M.	3.3.17	DOW
Muncey, Pte J.H.T.	29.9.18	KIA	Robertson, Pte A.F.	20.7.16	KIA
Nagel, Pte C.H.	26.9.17	DOW	Robertson, Pte T.	15.10.17	KIA
Naylor, Pte R.W.	26.4.18	KIA	Robertson, Pte W.B.	13.2.17	KIA
Nevinson, L–Cpl J.W.	1.10.18	KIA	Rochester, Pte T.J.	25.4.18	KIA
Newman, Pte P.A.	4.8.16	CS	Roderick, Pte D.	28.1.17	KIA
Noonan, Pte T.F.	25.9.17	KIA	Rogers, Pte C.C.	26.9.17	KIA
Northill, Pte T.J.	4.3.18	KIA	Rogers, Pte R.C.	25.9.17	KIA
Nunweek, Pte H.	27.10.17	KIA	Rooney, Pte E.T.	7.4.18	DOW
Oakes, Pte C.H.	26.4.18	KIA	Rosendale, Pte J.	15.7.16	KIA
O'Brien, Pte J.J.	27.9.17	KIA	Rossborough, Pte W.	25.9.17	KIA
O'Brien, Pte M.	15.10.18	DOW	Round, Pte W.A.	22.9.16	KIA
O'Brien, Pte R.	20.8.18	DOW	Rowley, Pte T.M.	16.3.17	DOW
O'Callaghan, Pte T.	26.9.17	KIA	Rudd, Pte W.	2.2.17	KIA
O'Connor, Pte T.H.	13.2.17	KIA	Russell, L–Cpl G.	3.9.16	DOW
O'Donnell, Pte E.	19.8.16	KIA	Rutter, Pte R.W.J.	12.2.18	DOS
Oliver, Pte C.F.	17.9.17	KIA	Ryan, Pte EJ.	25.9.17	KIA
(also known as Finchley)			Ryan, Pte J.L.	12.7.18	KIA
Orr, Pte J.J.	25.4.18	KIA	Ryan, Pte P.J.	15.7.16	KIA
Pace, Pte H.T.	26.9.17	KIA	Ryan, Pte P.J.	1.10.18	DOW
Packham, Pte F.	26.9.17	KIA	Salt, Pte B.P.	8.8.18	KIA
Palmer, L–Sgt H.K.	24.3.17	KIA	Saltau, L–Cpl B.J.	15.3.17	KIA
Parker, Pte G.T.	25.2.18	DOW	Santilla, Pte W.J.	26.4.18	KIA
Paterson, L–Cpl H.B.	23.8.18	KIA	Savolainen, Pte A.J.	20.7.16	KIA
Peart, Pte J.M.	30.9.16	KIA	Scott, Pte C.S.	26.9.17	KIA
Pengelly, Pte H.J.	26.9.17	KIA	Scott, Pte T.G.	8.8.18	KIA
(also known as Smith)			Scrieck, Pte H.R.	24.3.17	KIA
Penna, Pte W.C.F.	19.8.16	KIA	(also known as Rogers)		
Perkins, Pte A.E.	12.5.17	KIA	Sedgman, Pte W.H.	2.10.18	DOW
Pickering, Pte F.A.	9.8.18	DOW	Shanahan, Sgt W.	27.4.18	DOW
Pierson, Pte J.F.	18.8.16	KIA	Shand, Pte J.B.	5.4.18	KIA
Platt, Pte E.	23.5.18	NK	Shelton, Pte L.F.	26.9.17	KIA
Pollock, Pte A.	21.2.19	DOD	Shepherd, Pte F.C.	15.7.16	KIA
Pont, Pte N.F.	26.12.16	NK	Shields, Pte A.	28.1.17	KIA
Prow, Pte C.V.	26.9.17	KIA	Shore, Pte A.H.	17.5.18	DOW
Pryse, Pte A.L.	15.7.16	DOW	Short, CSM J.S.	5.4.18	KIA
Pugh, Pte J.R.	4.2.19	DOS	Shrimpton, Pte W.T.	15.10.17	KIA
Pyne, Pte F.	12.5.17	KIA	Silcock, Pte E.J.	4.7.18	KIA
Quade, Cpl W.	19.8.16	KIA	Simons, Pte D.L.	22.11.16	DOW
Quigg, Pte W.M.	2.2.17	KIA	Simons, Pte J.J.	20.7.16	KIA
Quinlan, Pte J.J.	28.10.17	DOW	Simpson, Pte S.H.	7.9.17	DOS
Rathbone, Pte G.E.T.	26.10.17	DOW	Simpson, Pte W.H.	6.7.18	KIA

Sizer, Pte A.A.	28.11.16	KIA	Turner, Pte W.E.	26.9.17	KIA
Sizer, Pte A.J.	12.12.16	KIA	Uglow, Pte A.H.	8.8.18	KIA
Skene, Pte G.A.	8.8.18	KIA	Vickers, Pte E.W.J.	1.10.18	DOW
Slattery, Pte C.P.T.	26.9.17	KIA	Vine, Pte R.V.B.	15.10.17	KIA
Smith, Pte E.	2.4.17	KIA	Wallace, Pte H.E.	11.5.17	KIA
Smith, Pte H.F.	25.4.18	KIA	Wallace, QMS J.C.	30.11.18	AK
Smith, Pte R.	26.9.17	KIA	(also known as Gilmour, J.C.)		
Smith, Pte W.G.	28.10.16	KIA	Walsh, Pte J.P.	21.7.18	KIA
Solano, Pte W.	14.4.18	DOS	Walter, Pte J.	25.9.17	KIA
Solomano, Pte F.J.	27.9.17	KIA	Walters, Pte G.E.	27.9.18	KIA
Spedding, Pte H.	28.8.18	KIA	Walters, Pte W.H.	26.9.17	KIA
Spiller, Pte R.S.	30.9.18	KIA	Warburton, Pte W.J.	26.9.17	KIA
Stanford, Pte J.	1.10.17	DOW	Ward, Pte G.R.	26.3.17	DOW
Steet, Pte A.	4.7.18	DOW	Warnock, Cpl R.	24.3.17	KIA
Stephens, Pte T.J.	7.8.16	KIA	Watson, Sgt A.	8.8.18	KIA
Stephenson, Cpl R.T.	2.10.18	DOW	Watt, Pte J.	27.9.17	KIA
Stewart, Pte G.W.	27.9.17	KIA	Weir, Pte R.R.	25.9 17	KIA
Stewart, Pte J. McA.	3.4.17	KIA	Wells, Pte F.E.	24.6 16	DOS
Stone, Sgt C.C.	12.5.17	KIA	Wellstead, Pte W.G.	30.9.18	KIA
Stone, Pte L.	7.10.18	DOW	Westgarth, Pte R.F.	24.3.17	KIA
Strahan, Sgt A.	20.7.16	DOW	Whillance, Pte B.G.	27.9.17	KIA
Strahan, Pte C.E.	12.5.17	KIA	White, Pte A.	26.9.17	KIA
Stranger, Pte F.	22.3.18	DOW	Williams, Cpl W.J.	6.12.17	KIA
Street, Pte H.H.S.	5.3.18	KIA	Williams, L-Cpl E.C.	15.8.16	DOW
Sullivan, CSM H.P.	16.8.18	DOW	Williams, L-Cpl W.	5.4.18	DOW
Sweeney, Pte N.J.	22.9.16	KIA	Williams, Pte F.J.	14.12.17	KIA
Symons, Pte S.T.	9.3.18	DOW	Williams, Pte W.S.	26.9 17	KIA
Tavener, Pte A.	29.9.18	KIA	Williamson, Pte J.	25.9 17	KIA
(also known as Curran, A.)			Willis, Pte T.N.	26.9.17	KIA
Taylor, Pte A.	25.9.17	DOW	Willoughby, Pte A.S.B.	27.9.17	KIA
Taylor, Pte T.	28.10.17	DOW	Wilson, Pte B.G.	5.3.18	KIA
Temple, Pte H.	16.7.16	KIA	Wilson, Pte J.H.	26.9.17	KIA
Tennant, Pte G.	1.9.18	KIA	Wilson, Pte M.	16.7.18	DOD
Thomas, Pte L.G.	30.9.18	DOW	Winter, Pte H.W.	20.3.17	KIA
Thompson, L-Cpl F.N.	24.6.18	DOW	Wise, Pte H.M.	25.2.18	KIA
Thompson, Pte J.F.	1.10.18	KIA	Worland, L-Cpl A.R.	6.4.18	DOW
Thorn, Pte W.T.	25.4.18	KIA	Woollett, Pte R.	5.4.18	KIA
Thurston, Pte S.	26.5.18	KIA	Wright, L-Cpl J.R.	26.11.16	DOW
Timms, A/Cpl A.H.	25.3.17	DOW	Wyeth, Pte W.G.	25.9.17	KIA
Tognolini, Pte J.	25.4.18	KIA	Young, Pte A J.	30.8.18	KIA
Tull, Pte C.	16.3.17	NK	Zimmer, Pte W.H.	17.6.18	KIA
Turlan, Pte L.H.A.	5.4.18	KIA			
Turnbull, Pte A.F.	11.8.18	DOW			

Survivors
57th Battalion 1916 — 1918

ABBOTT HE
ABBOTT LJ
ABBOTT RR
ADAMS CWA
ADAMS EJ
ADAMS H
ADAMS P
ADAMS WG
ADLER JE
AITCHISON RMC
AKERS AL
AKERS B
AKERS JW
ALCOCK WG
ALEXEJEW AA
ALFORD J
ALFORD LS
ALLAN HM
ALLAN PA
ALLEN CH
ALLEN E
ALLEN FJ
ALLEN GS
ALLEN JG
ALLEN RA
ALLEN WJ
ALSOP J
ANDERSON GW
ANDERSON H
ANDERSON HC
ANDERSON J
ANDERSON JW
ANDERSON R
ANDERSON RD
ANDERSON W
ANDREWS FF
ANDREWS H
ANDREWS M
ANDREWS W
ANGUS CJ
APIANO T
APPLETON G
(also known as
G Smith)
ARCHER H
ARCHER WJ
ARKELL FH
ARLAND JE

ARMSTRONG EJ
ARMSTRONG G
ARNOTT R
ARQUELLO D
ASHFORD A
ASHLEY EA
ASHMORE HE
ASHMORE J
ATHERTON B
ATKINS AV
ATKINS EL
ATKINS G
ATKINS HEG
ATKINS REA
ATKINS S
ATKINSON EK
ATKINSON EW
ATKINSON G
ATKINSON JW
AULD A
AUSTIN ES
AUSTIN H
AUSTIN H
AYRE J
BAGER M
BAILEY GW
BAILEY HE
BAILEY W
BAKER A
BAKER L
BAKER NR
BAKER SN
BAKER T
BALDWIN JM
BALFOUR RJ
BANFIELD GW
BANKIER JW
BANNISTER H
BARBER HL
BARCLAY WE
BARHAM RW
BARKER EW
BARKER HE
BARKER RC
BARKER SH
BARNES AE
BARRITT MJ
BARRON JG

BARTHELSON AM
BARTLETT JM
BARTLEY JJ
BARTON HG
BARTRIM EJ
BASKIVILLE WHJ
BASSETT TJ
BATCHELOAR H
BATE A
BATES JJ
BATTY FP
BATTYE F
BAUL GE
BAXTER GE
BAXTER H
BAZLEY F
BEARD FE
BEARE E
BEASLEY AJ
BEAUFORT J
BECKETT C
BEER GJ
BEGG JA
BEGGS AE
BEGLEY JHF
BEITH B McN
BELL A
BELL C
BELL GD
BELL J
BELL JC
BELL LW
BELL WG
BELLAMMY EA
BELMONT F
BENEY FH
BENN JJ
BENNETT JL
BENNETT WW
BENNIE RJ
BENOIT T
BENSON JO
BENTON J
BERRIGAN A
BERRY A
BEST RSC
BETTINELLI JT
BEVERIDGE T

BICE HM
BIER A
BILLSON HJ
BIRCH JE
BIRCH RS
BIRD J
(also known as
H W Lingard)
BIRDSEY B
BIRKETT WH
BIRNIE GH
BIRTHISEL JR
BIRTHISEL WS
BISHOP J
BISKE H
BISSET W
BISSETT JA
BLACK J
BLACK J
BLACKBURN AW
BLACKLOCK WJ
BLACKWELL FW
BLAKE A
BLAKE RS
BLANDFORD G
BLANDTHORN AH
BLEASDALE HW
BLESSLEY HWD
BLIGHT GA
BLISS CA
BLOSSETT W
BOLAND FW
BOLAND M
BOLITHO M
BOLLMEYER CH
BONE CLG
BONNETT HJ
BOON HDR
BOOTH HA
BOOTH WE
BOOTHROYD F
BORDEN H
BOSSEN AH
BOSWELL H
BOTTRILL SA
BOUCHER HS
BOURKE A
BOURKE A

BOWBRIDGE A
BOWEN WH
BOWRING CG
BOWYER SN
BOXSHALL AV
BOYCE J
BOYCE DH
BOYD A
BOYD J
BOYLE HW
BOYLE TD
BRADFORD SR
BRADY G
BRAITHWAITE CR
BRAMLEY KG
BRANNAGAN CE
BRAWN JG
BRAY J
BRAZIER THC
BRAZZEL S
BREEZE JN
BRENNAN JA
BREWER DH
BRIDGELAND AW
BRIGGS AR
BRIGGS H
BRIGGS J
BRIGHT HM
BRINTON EE
BRISTER EW
BRITTEN CF
BRODIE DA
BROOKS E
BROOMHAM S
BROPHY CFJ
BROWN AHF
BROWN AJ
BROWN FH
BROWN FJ
BROWN FW
BROWN GEL
BROWN GJ
BROWN JG
BROWN H
BROWN J
BROWN S
BROWN WD
BROWN WE
BROWN WF
BROWN WL
BROWNING HE
BROWNING WJ
BRUCE CE
BRUNEL CJ

BRUTON AA
BRYANS TF
BUBB AE
BUCHANAN HJ
BUCK AJ
BUCKLAND D
BUCKLEY J
BUCKLEY LJ
BUCKMASTER WJ
BULL CC
BULL H
BULL S
BURCHALL FR
BURCHETT W
BURDON BR
BURKE E
BURKE JF
BURKE MJ
BURKE P
BURNETT MG
BURNS AP
BURNS WA
BURRELL A
BURROWES A
BURROWS EC
BURROWS EJ
BURROWS EM
BURTON F
BURTON JA
BUTCHER HD
BUTLER SO
BUTLER W
BUTTERS RW
BYRNES JA
BYRON JR
CADDEN JW
CAIN EE
CAIRNS AR
CALDWELL JJ
CALE TG
CALLAWAY AE
CALLAWAY TA
CAMERON A
CAMERON CAE
CAMERON EJ
CAMERON WJ
CAMPBELL H
CAMPBELL J
CAMPBELL N
CAMPBELL N
CAMPBELL R
CANN GA
CANTWELL WH
CARAGHER W

CARE DC
CARELESS HE
CARELESS HE
CARMAN JH
CARMICHAEL K
CARNE P
CARNEGIE WB
CAROLAN PJ
CARR M
CARRINGTON G
CARROLL AJ
CARROLL J
CARROLL WH
CARRUTHERS D
CARRUTHERS FW
CARSON WV
CARTER DC
CARTER HH
CARTER JC
CASEY F
CASEY WP
CASHMAN RJ
CASHMERE CJ
CASLEY JH
CHADWICK F
CHALKER LD
CHALKER SA
CHALMERS RD
CHANDLER EJ
CHANDLER RH
CHAPMAN HN
CHAPMAN RK
CHARLES WF
CHARLTON W
CHARTERIS HB
CHEESEMAN RE
CHENERY GG
CHESHER WH
CHETTLE H
CHURCH AH
CHURCH RE
CLANCY SJ
CLAPTON SM
CLARK AJ
CLARK PA
CLARKE GR
CLAYTON G
CLAYTON G
CLUCAS WR
CLUTTERBUCK HR
COATES G
COCKRAM L
COCHRANE EJ
COCHRANE RS

COCKRANE WS
COFFEY WT
COHEN AV
COLE EW
COLEMAN HV
COLLTT CH
COLLETT P
COLLETT W
COLLINGBURN FH
COLLINS EF
COLLINS JH
COLLINS JJ
COLLINS P
COLLINS W
COLLISTER HNF
COLLIVER ECV
COLNAN C
COLSON GT
COLVIN GD
COMEY E
COMINI T
COMTE PC
CONLEY J
CONNELL WH
CONNELLY JJ
CONNIFF MJ
CONNOLLY H
COOK AB
COOK CJ
COOK JF
COOKE EJ
COOKE GN
COOMBS HS
COOPER D
COOPER G
COOPER GW
COOPER F
COOPER FJ
COOPER JF
COOPER JF
COOTS JW
CORBETT GA
CORBETT WF
CORBETT WM
CORCORAN WJ
CORFE LC
CORKER MH
CORNELL C
CORNEY E
COSTELLO AJT
COTTON JS
COUCH S
COUGHLAN D
COULSTON TH

198

COUTIE EE
COWAN H
COW LJ
COWLEY F
COWLING F
COWLING RH
COX A
COX AH
CRICHTON F
CRIGAN AH
CRIGAN J
CRIGAN WC
CRIPPS AW
CROCKER VAJ
CROCKETT CH
CROFT H
CROFT JH
CROFTS AR
CROSS WJ
CROUCH SHF
CROUCH WSB
CRUMPLER NF
CUBBINS LJL
CULLEN LT
CUMMINGS H
CUNNINGHAM G
CUNNINGHAM H
CURE W
CURNOW LJ
CURNOW WT
CURRAN JC
CURRAN LA
CURRIE A
CURRIE F
CURRIE FCE
CURRIE HN
CURRIE JE
CURRIE MH
CURRIE W
CURRIE W
CURRY W
CURTAIN JJ
CURTIS C
CURTIS HD
CURTIS WG
CURTIS WJ
CUTTING CD
DABONDE P
DAISH LG
DALGLEISH CK
DALGLEISH WR
DANSEY RB
DARCY DE
DARKER GW

DARKER W
DART LF
DART WJ
DAVENPORT GN
DAVENPORT HA
DAVENPORT W
DAVERN DC
DAVEY CA
DAVEY EC
DAVEY WJ
DAVIDSON HL
DAVIDSON JL
DAVIDSON PT
DAVIDSON R
DAVIE JG
DAVIES CL
DAVIES D
DAVIES FC
DAVIES W
DAVIES W
DAVIES WD
DAVIS AJ
DAVIS AP
DAVIS AT
DAVIS AV
DAVIS CH
DAVIS CW
DAVIS RD
DAVIS WE
DAWSON EF
DAWSON H
DAWSON J
DAWSON WG
DAWSON WS
DAY H
DAY JH
DAY LA
DE CAMPO NL
DE FOREST JJ
DE LASTIE CJ
DEAN G
DEAN G
DEAN RL
DEAN W
DEANE EC
DEEGAN JJ
DEHNE HH
DEHNE WE
DELAHUNTY JR
DENCH AW
DENEHY CA
DENISON WJ
DENNETT FE
DENNEY FC

DENNING GC
DENNIS WJ
DENT WJ
DERHAM W
DERRICK C
DEVEREAUX LF
DEVLIN FM
DEWHIRST JT
DIAPER WW
DICKENSON HC
DICKENSON JEG
DICKINSON HJ
DICKSON J
DILLON GM
DINEEN AC
DIXON RW
DOBBIN HA
DOBBIN MJ
DOBBINSON W
DOBIE A
DOBSON H
DOCHERTY JC
DODD WE
DOLAN CRL
DONALDSON JW
DONNELLY JD
DONNISON A
DONOHOE J
DONOVAN CJ
DONOVAN R
DOOHAN JMcR
DORRINGTON CC
DOUTREBAND R
DOW W
DOWLIN RT
DOWLING G
DOWNING F
DOWNING WH
DOYLE JH
DOYLE T
DRAFFIN JT
DRAGE FR
DREWETT WHG
DRISCOLL RF
DRUMMIE JL
DRUMMOND DG
DRUMMOND R
DRUMMOND WS
DRYSDALE RH
DUCKETT JP
DUCKLING AA
DUFFY JS
DUGGAN LJP
DUKE J

DUMBLE EG
DUNCAN GD
DUNCAN JT
DUNCAN RS
DUNCOMBE A
DUNDEN FA
DUNMORE W
DUNN H
DUNN HH
DUNN VC
DUNN WS
DURNO LA
DURSTON AJ
DURSTON FH
DUTHIE CA
DWYER DV
EADIE HE
EARL J
EASTBROOK RT
EATHER GC
EBBS ERH
EBDON AC
EDGAR LD
EDGAR WES
EDGERTON A
EDWARDS GA
EDWARDS HA
EDWARDS T
EDWARDSEN H
ELCOCK WT
ELLARD CR
ELLES AG
ELLIOTT JJ
ELLIOTT LW
ELLIOTT RJ
ELLIS L
ELLIS WH
ELLSON ST
ELPHICK FB
ELSDEN H
ENGELLENNER SH
ENGLAND EM
ENNOR JC
ERREY GA
ESSING CW
ESSON W
EVANS J
EVANS R
EVANS RS
EVANS T
EYLES AC
FAIRLESS ELR
FAIRLIE WT
FAIRMAN GS

FALCONER D
FALCONER LJ
FALLA A
FALLON N
FANANCE A
FARGHER M
FARRANT G
FARRELL HR
FARRELL T
FARRINGTON W
FAULKNER CT
FAYEN AR
FEARON WHM
FEATHERSTONE WE
FENNER PW
FENTON WEH
FERGUSON PF
FERRES HDG
FIELD N
FIELDER G
FILES EH
FILMER AG
FIRTH RA
FISHER EE
FISHER J
(also known as
J F Van de Vun)
FISK WH
FITCH LR
FITHALL AWL
FITZGERALD EE
FITZGERALD ML
FITZGERALD PJ
FITZPATRICK CE
FLAHERTY JA
FLANAGAN PW
FLATT A
FLATT H
FLAVELL W
FLEMING GH
FLEMING JH
FLETCHER AG
FLETCHER LJ
FLETCHER S
FLIGHT GR
FLYNN JP
FOGARTY JH
FOLEY CA
FOLLETT CL
FOOT MT
FOOTE FE
FORBES J
FORBES LO
FORBES R

FORD GE
FORD GR
FORD HE
FORD J
FORDE JJ
FORDHAM LR
FORREST CG
FORREST GW
FORRESTER GA
FORRESTER S
FOSTER EV
FOSTER JA
FOWLER JH
FOWLER KE
FOWLER WE
FRANCE SE
FRANKLIN AV
FRASER HA
FRASER S
FREEMAN DL de C
FREEMAN GR
FREEMAN JA
FRENCH CC
FRENCH LE
FREW B
FREY AJ
FRYER GT
FULLER TAD
FULLER W
FUNNELL AFJ
GALLAGHER J
GALLAHER AA
GALLUS W
GALVIN PJ
GAMBLE R
GANT EW
GARDEN LN
GARDINER AL
GARDINER FS
GARDINER WH
GARLICK AA
GARRETT LA
GARTSIDE SAZ
GASH RA
GATES EN
GAUT EW
GEARY BJ
GEARY P
GEORGE EA
GEORGE T
GERMAINE JF
GEYER LM
GIBBONS W
GIBBS AEE

GIBBS R
GIBSON R
GILBERT CF
GILES AT
GILES JH
GILLARD P
GILMORE FW
GIRLEY L
GIRVAN E
GLASS HW
GLEESON HWB
GLEN JS
GLENISTER PJ
GLOG L
GODBER AE
GODDARD WJW
GOFF AG
GOLDSWORTHY G
GOODALL SG
GOODARE T
GOODLETT A
GOODWIN AH
GOODWIN C
GOODWIN RH
GORDON AEJ
GORDON WR
GOREY EH
GOREY M
GORRINGE ELJ
GOSS C
GOWDIE WA
GRAHAM CS
GRAHAM DDB
GRAHAM E
GRAHAM J
GRAHAM RE
GRANT CHB
GRANT JG
GRANT MC
GRAY HT
GRAY JW
GRAY SL
GRAYSTONE HM
GREEN A
GREEN EA
GREEN GR
GREEN JD
GREEN T
GREENING EJ
GREENMAN A
GREENWAY FD
GREIG AS
GREIG GM
GRENDA GF

GRESTY F
GRICE CS
GRIEVE AL
GRIFFIN S
GRIFFIN W
GRIFFITHS CH
GRIFFITHS G
GRIFFITHS SR
GROOBY A
GUILMARTIN TGC
GULEY L
GUNDRY WJ
HACLEY G
HADDEN TC
HADSON J
HAFFA HW
HAGELUND LA
HAINES NF
HALE HR
HALE WG
HALL AH
HALL EM
HALL J
HALL M
HALL T
HALPIN PJ
HAMILTON F
HAMILTON FA
HAMILTON MF
HAMILTON RB
HAMILTON RH
HAMPTON A
HANDCOCK F
HANN B
HANN CA
HANNAN MJ
HANNAN WJ
HANSEN HJ
HANSEN NHE
HANSFORD RW
HARBOUR HJH
HARDBATTLE GW
HARDING HW
HARDINGHAM JD
HARDRIDGE AB
HARDY ET
HARGRAVES JA
HARGREAVES GH
HARLE T
HARLEY WL
HARLOW TH
HARPER A
HARRINGTON CV
HARRINGTON TC

HARRIS AG
HARRIS AT
HARRIS GE
HARRIS J
HARRIS RA
HARRIS WC
HARRISON PC
HARRISON WR
HART DW
HART WF
HARTIGAN J
HARVEY G
HARVEY LRA
HARVEY MJ
HATCH FS
HATFIELD EK
HAUSEN GE
HAWKINS AG
HAWKSWORTH J
HAYES B
HAYES CJH
HAYES D
HAYES HW
HAYES WH
HAYMAN N
HAYWARD G
HAZELL JB
HEDBERG CP
HEDLEY CP
HEFFER FE
HEFFORD R
HEITMANN FE
HEMLEY WO
HENDERSON CH
HENDERSON CH
HENDERSON CW
HENDRICK M
HENDRICKSON J
HENWOOD WG
HERCULES JW
HERCULES RA
HERIOT N
HERON D
HERRICK FR
HESSE PR
HEWBER A
HEWSTON W
HIGGINS JJ
HILDITCH LW
HILL C
HILL F
HILL HE
HILL WCF
HILTON JT

HINCHCLIFFE CW
HINDLEY FG
HOBART CG
HOBBS AG
HOCKING HJ
HOCKING RJ
HODDINOTT WE
HODGE JMC
HODGES CK
HODGES JE
HODKINSON OD
HODSON CP
HODSON J
HOFF JT
HOGAN TF
HOKANSON AH
HOLDOM LA
HOLDSWORTH WR
HOLLAND FJ
HOLLAND G
HOLLAND HC
HOLLAND R
HOLLEY G
HOLLOWAY WT
HOLMES CA
HOLMES E
HOLMES H
HOLMES W
HOLOPHY JP
HOLT EG
HOMER GV
HOMER GV
HOMEWOOD LC
HONEY SG
HOOD JA
HOOPER AR
HOPE RA
HOPGOOD F
HOPPER EA
HOPPING CH
HORE J
HORE LG
HORNBY HG
HORRIGAN TP
HORSBRUGH DW
HOSIE H
HOSKING BP
HOUGHTON W
HOWDEN WH
HOWELL G
HOWELL K
HOWES OW
HUBBLE RS
HUGHES AC

HUGHES F
HUGHES FR
HUGHES FV
HUGHES JH
HUNT E
HUNTER J
HUNTER RW
HUNTER WD
HUON GLV
HURLAM A
HUTCHINSON AL
HUTCHINSON J
HUTCHINSON R
HUTHNANCE PBE
HUTSON FAW
HUTSON HS
HUTTON JM
IDDLES EJ
IDDLES EJ
IDDLES H
ILES G
ILES TA
IMRIE DW
INGLE WH
INIFER LG
ISBEL F
ISHERWOOD EC
IVORY EH
JACKA A
JACOBSON FJ
JAMES GT
JAMES TE
JAMES W
JAMIESON JJ
JAMIESON KS
JAMIESON WT
JANSEN BT
JASON HC
JEBB C
JEFFCOTT JR
JEFFERY AO
JEFFERY CF
JEFFERY S
JENKINS CR
JENKINS GM
JENNINGS GS
JENNINGS R
JENSEN NA
JERRAM LR
JESSUP FJ
JINNETTE P
JOHNSON FE
JOHNSON J
JOHNSON JA

JOHNSON PW
JOHNSON WW
JOHNSTON J
JOHNSTON RG
JOHNSTONE W
JOHNSTONE WJ
JOLLIFFE HD
JONES BJ
JONES D
JONES DF
JONES DW
JONES F
JONES G
JONES GJ
JONES HP
JONES LH
JONES OC
JONES W
JONES W
JORDAN CL
JOSEPH LC
JOYCE D
JOYCE PC
KAHLER JG
KAVANAGH J
KAVANAGH JJ
KAY J
KAYVETT RH
KEANE TL
KEARNS JJ
KEARON RE
KEATING RG
KEDDIE BJ
KEDDIE OW
KEITH F
KELLCHER J
KELLEHER M
KELLEHER M
KELLEY J
KELLY B
KEMP A
KEMP E
KEMP E
KENDALL AWJ
KENEALY FJ
KENLEY RJ
KENNEDY C
KENNEDY JT
KENNEDY S
KENTISH CH
KERR AW
KERR DW
KERR G
KERR GMcD

KERR H
KERR M
KERR PV
KERR T
KERR WW
KESTER F
KEYS AE
KEYS EK
KIDD EB
KIERNAN AR
KIERNAN J
KILDUFF WJ
KILGOUR RJ
KILGOUR W
KILKELLY JB
KILLEEN CM
KILMARTIN G
KILPATRICK JT
KIMBER E
KIMPTON EW
KING A
KING F
KING HG
KING HR
KING J
KING J
KING JA
KING S
KING W
KING WA
KING WH
KINSMAN HS
KINSMORE JW
KIRBY EA
KIRBY JS
KIRBY PV
KIRKHAM A
KIRKHAM B
KIRWAN PJ
KITCHEN AJ
KITCHEN HL
KITCHER CE
KITTO HTJ
KLEIN BI
KNIGHT A
KNIGHT HJ
KNIGHT J
KNIGHT J
KNIGHT R
KNOX DG
KNUCKEY WJ
KRISTIANSEN O
LABBAN WA
LACK ATF

LACK RE
LACY SR
LADGROVE TSC
LAING JB
LAKE JC
LAMBERT JH
LAMBERT L
LANDER E
LANE A
LANE LH
LANE OL
LANE SWB
LANG DG
LANGLEY R
LANIGAN W
LANYON JJ
LARKINS WE
LARRAD ARB
LARRAD G
LARSON AP
LAUDER E
LAUGHTON GI
LAWLER DFP
LAWRENCE JL
LAWSON AW
LAWSON CJ
LAWSON J
LAWSON JS
LAY FHE
LAYH HTC
LAYTON J
LE BROCK DT
LEAR C
LEAR L
LEDGERTON W
LEE HA
LEE P
LEEMING HH
LEEVIS WC
LEGGETT WT
LEHMANN EH
LEITCH AP
LEITCH WHC
LEMIN A
LENNON H
LEONARD MJ
LESLIE J
LETHLEAN HJT
LEVER GCH
LEVITT WEJ
LEVY CJ
LEWIS AI
LEWIS HJ
LEWIS JE

LEWIS RJ
LEWIS RW
LEWIS V
LEWIS WAA
LEWIS WC
LICAS PC
LIDDELL
LIDDICUT A
LIDDICUTT HG
LIDDY J
LILLIS JA
LINDREA A
LINDSAY TF
LINTON RV
LINZ PH
LITTLE A
LITTLE LW
LIVCO WH
LIVING AJ
LLOYD SF
LOBBAN KI
LOCK AST
LOCK JH
LOFT JC
LONG J
LONG J
LONG LE
LONG WA
LORD HW
LORIMER EV
LOUGHLIN JE
LOUGHREN GE
LOVE JW
LOY JS
LUCAS EJ
LUCAS NC
LUCAS SE
LUIGARD HW
LUNDGREN GW
LUNN G
LUTCH AP
LYALL FH
LYNCH EW
LYNCH WH
LYNDON HR
LYONS R
MacDERMOTT GH
MacFARLANE GS
MacFARLANE HT
MACK J
MACKAY DG
MACKAY WDS
MacKELLAR RE
MACKEN CA

MACKIE JM
MACKINTOSH C
MACLEOD JN
MACPHERSON HD
MADDAMS T
MADDEN G
MAHER D
MAHER EA
MAHER F
MAHER L
MAHER L
MAHER T
MAHONEY JA
MAJOR JSW
MAKEPEACE AT
MALLATT CT
MALLOWES GE
MALONE PB
MALONEY AE
MALONEY E
MANN F
MANN W
MANSER RT
MANSFIELD HS
MANSFIELD L
MARCHANT WE
MARR J
MARRIOTT AS
MARSH FE
MARSH GM
MARSHALL AE
MARSHALL G
MARSHALL N
MARSHALL TA
MARSHALL W
MARTIN AR
MARTIN E
MARTIN G
MARTIN JA
MARTIN JA
MARTIN JH
MARTIN JL
MARTIN PW
MARTIN T
MARTIN WF
MASKELL A
MASON FW
MASON HL
MASON PW
MASSEY FJ
MATHIESON TH
MATHIESON WR
MATTHEWSON HB
MAY F

202

MAY T
MAY WJ
MAYNARD CWL
McALPINE RS
McAULAY DR
McAULEY M
McBAIN CF
McCALLUM JG
McCARTHY GW
McCARTHY JA
McCAY NJ
McCHRYSTAL D
McCOLL D
McCOLL KR
McCONNELL E
McCONNELL J
McCONNELL WA
McCONNELL WJ
McCORKELL FJ
McCORKELLE RW
McCORMICK HS
McCREA DA
McCREA HA
McCOLLOCK AW
McCURDY JA
McDERMOTT RJ
McDONALD A
McDONALD AC
McDONALD AR
McDONALD D
McDONALD D
McDONALD DJ
McDONALD G
McDONALD H
McDONALD HA
McDONALD J
McDONALD JA
McDONALD JJ
McDONALD JR
McDONALD L
McDONALD R
McDONALD WHL
McDONOUGH SB
McEVOY J
McEWAN FA
McFARLANE D
McFARLANE HS
McFARLANE RD
McFARLANE RJ
McFARLANE W
McGEORGE R
McGORLICK J
McGREGOR JF
McINNES ADE

McINTOSH JW
McINTOSH R
McIVER JJ
McIVER M
McIVER P
McIVER T
McKAY GS
McKAY MR
McKAY R
McKAY W
McKAY WJ
McKELVIE FW
McKENNA JJ
McKENNA T
McKENZIE AJ
McKENZIE DM
McKENZIE O
McKENZIE OP
McKENZIE P
McKEOWN W
McKIBBIN J
McKIBBIN JJ
McKINLAY NL
McKINSTRY AH
McLAWS KJ
McLEAN A
McLEISH JAW
McLEOD AC
McLEOD DE
McLEOD N
McLEOD NC
McMASTER A
McMILLAN J
McMILLAN R
McNAMARA JP
McNAMEE TJ
McNEIL H
McNULTY JE
McPHAIL AJ
McPHAIL NA
McPHERSON AJ
McPHERSON J
McPHERSON JRA
McPHERSON RD
McQUITTY JL
McSWAIN A
McVEIGH HV
McWHANNELL FB
MEADE TJ
MEAGER A
MEAGER BCW
MEARA WJ
MEGARRITY RK
MEGGS L

MEIGAN RH
MELEN RC
MENZIES E
MEREDITH VJ
MERRIFIELD GD
MESSINA CG
MIBLER JMcD
MILDWATER OV
MILGATE SA
MILLARD AA
MILLARD SA
MILLER AC
MILLER AR
MILLER JD
MILLER NH
MILLER R
MILLER R
MILLER WA
MILLER WK
MILLS RS
MILLS TJ
MITCHELL A
MITCHELL GH
MITCHELL JP
MOLONY J
MONAGHAN AW
MONEY AJ
MONEY C
MONEY WA
MONK L
MONKS CF
MOODIE LW
MOODY FJ
MOON CL
MOON W
MOONEY SV
MOORE C
MOORE EJ
MOORE HGQ
MOORE JR
MORGAN JC
MORGAN JJ
MORLEY WA
MORRIS DA
MORRIS E
MORRIS JL
MORRIS KD
MORRIS LF
MORRIS P
MORRISON A
MORRISON C
MORRISON D
MORRISON HCA
MORRISON KJ

MORRISON WR
MORRISON WS
MORROW TW
MORTON L
MOSS WJ
MOULDER CJ
MOUNTJOY C
MOUNTNEY WR
MOXHAM A
MOXON RWG
MULLEN EV
MULLETT RE
MUNRO DP
MUNSON JB
MUNTZ ATB
MUNTZ WN
MURPHY D
MURPHY E
MURPHY EHS
MURPHY FE
MURPHY J
MURPHY J
MURPHY JH
MURPHY JL
MURPHY L
MURPHY M
MURPHY P
MURPHY W
MURRAY JM
MURTAGH J
MUSTON W
MUTIMER SG
MUXWORTHY T
NAISH W
NANCARROW AC
NAPIER G
NEASON J
NEILD SMB
NEILSON PS
NELSON D
NELSON HH
NELSON JP
NELSON VJ
NELSON WW
NESBIT JJ
NESBITT WG
NEWELL A
NEWELL TF
NEWMAN WG
NEWTON H
NEWTON JW
NEWTON MJ
NEWTON N
NICHOL SJ

NICHOLL AF
NICHOLL CS
NICHOLLS AJ
NICHOLLS GW
NICHOLLS HV
NICHOLSON AMcK
NICHOLSON E
NICHOLSON EL
NICHOLSON L
NICHOLSON LA
NICHOLSON LH
NICHOLSON NJ
NICHOLSON W
NICHOLSON WR
NICKELSON RJ
NICOLL CP
NICOLL TK
NICOLLS JF
NOAD CSA
NOBLE T
NOLAN DP
NORMINGTON AS
NORRIS ER
NORRIS HG
NORRIS JS
NORWOOD WJ
NUGENT TC
NUTCHEY DC
O'BRIEN EC
O'BRIEN J
O'BRIEN JJ
O'BRIEN TF
O'BRYAN HJ
O'BRYAN TJ
O'CONNELL MK
O'CONNOR B
O'CONNOR D
O'CONNOR J
O'CONNOR JE
O'DONNELL SJJ
O'DWYER J
O'FLYNN M
O'HAGAN M
O'LEARY AJ
O'NEILL J
O'SULLIVAN F
OAKES AJ
OAKLEY AW
OATEN CH
OATES PO
ODGERS TJ
OFFERMAN WF
OHMAN VGO
OLD JS

OLDEN TH
OLIVER F
OLLEY EW
OLNEY FD
OLVER H
OOSSOFF F
ORAM AG
OSBORNE LS
OSBORNE R
OSBORNE WJ
OWEN RS
OWEN S
OWENS C
PACHOLLI WR
PACK DW
PAGE JF
PAGE JH
PANKHURST A
PARAMAN A
PARKER F
PARKER N
PARKINSON W
PARKINSON WG
PARKS GAT
PARR EO
PARRY AF
PARRY TG
PATERSON A
PATON JG
PATTEN W
PATTERSON AF
PATTERSON HA
PATTERSON RS
PAUL FE
PAULSEN GM
PAULSEN J
PEACOCK B
PEARCE AT
PEARCE HE
PEARSON JR
PEARSON T
PEART HD
PEGG E
PENMAN P
PENNY GC
PERRY JC
PERRY SH
PETERS G
PETERSEN ECB
PETERSON J
PETERSON SJ
PETTS AJ
PHILLIPS A
PHILLIPS CR

PHILLIPS GR
PHILLIPS JN
PHILLIPS PJG
PHILLIPS RK
PHILLIPS WS
PIBLADO J
PICKERING AJ
PICKERING H
PIGG EE
PINBLETT CJ
PINCHBECK R
PINDER JF
PITCHER BG
PITTS W
PIZZEY WC
PIZZY A
PLEDGE HL
PLENDERLEITH A
PLUNKETT EY
POCKINGTON WE
POLLARD R
PONTING RF
POTTER AE
POTTER FA
POTTER JH
POTTER TB
POULTER WJ
POVEY ET
PRATT SED
PREST PC
PRESTON CP
PRIDDEY AG
PRIMROSE JB
PRINCE R
PROCTOR R
PROWSE A
PRYOR JW
PUNTER GC
PURCELL PH
PURCELL TJ
PURKIS JA
PURVIS CS
PYE WL
QUARRELL TA
QUIN D
QUINLAN EJ
QUINN E
QUINN J
QUINTABA T
QUIRK WJ
RACHFORD J
RADCLIFFE HO
RAE FW
RAE RW

RAGLUS JW
RAMSAY AA
RAMSAY E
RAMSAY JD
RANSOM GH
RANSOM HF
RANSON FJ
RATCLIFFE LT
RAWLINGS BT
RAWLINGS S
RAWLINGS WJ
RAYNER CF
RAYNER WH
RAYSON H
READ CJ
READ RR
READ SE
REDDING AW
REDMOND LW
REED PG
REES J
REID J
REID J
REID J
REID NRA
REID RH
REID RN
REIS V
RENA JA
RENFREE RJ
RICARDO C
RICE CB
RICHARDS CT
RICHARDS F
RICHARDS GA
RICHARDS J
RICHARDS LC
RICHARDSON A
RICHARDSON FG
RICHARDSON J
RICKETTS HC
RIDDELL GT
RIDDELL RH
RIDDETT AEC
RIDGE J
RIGBYE GH
RILEY GR
RILEY LF
RITCHIE GJ
RITSON W
ROACH JH
ROBBINS W
ROBERTSON CD
ROBERTSON E

ROBERTSON GB
ROBERTSON GO
ROBERTSON JK
ROBINS T
ROBINS WM
ROBINSON C
ROBINSON GA
ROBINSON L
ROBINSON LD
ROBINSON LJ
ROBINSON TH
ROBINSON WJ
ROCHE LA
ROCKETT CH
ROCKETT WC
RODDA F
RODDY F
RODGERS DC
RODGERS JWL
RODGERS TSO
RODGERS WAL
RODONI JB
ROGERS CWT
ROGERS EC
ROHAN J
RONALD AF
ROPER DH
ROSS AG
ROSS AJW
ROSS CR
ROSS G
ROSS RC
ROSS RLC
ROSS WJ
ROSS WL
ROUSE AA
ROWBOTTOM RK
ROWE E
ROWE HJ
ROWE VM
ROWE WJ
ROWLEY GA
ROWORTH FS
ROYALS AH
RUDD VGM
RUDDUCK E
RUGLESS GF
RUSSELL WG
RUSSON A
RYAN CJ
RYAN J
RYAN JJ
RYAN LP
RYAN P

RYAN WHC
RYAN WJA
RYDER HJ
SALMON RA
SAMPSON AM
SAMS HC
SAMUELS CCB
SANDOE JBW
SANSON AJ
SARGEANT A
SAUNDERS GH
SAUNDERS S
SAUNDERS W
SAVAGE AJ
SAVILLE N
SAVILLE WG
SCANLON H
SCHLOTTERLEIN JA
SCHMAHL G
SCHMIDT LC
SCHOLFIELD J
SCHOLFIELD LN
SCRODER JD
SCHULTZ WJ
SCHUMACHER JT
SCOINES WH
SCOTT AP
SCOTT JA
SCOTT RW
SCOTT SS
SEDDON RD
SELBY KGM
SELLECK GG
SERPELL EW
SEYFARTH HA
SEYMOUR EW
SEYMOUR FB
SHADBOLT DE
SHANNON EJ
SHARP HS
SHARP T
SHARPLES RJ
SHAW A
SHAW F
SHEARER RJL
SHEEAN CL
SHEEDY SH
SHEPHERD R
SHEPHERD RJ
SHEPPARD FM
SHERRY JWH
SHERWELL WG
SHILLING J
SHIPP J

SHIPPARD EL
SHORE S
SHUTER SC
SHUTTLEWORTH H
SIDDINS JT
SIM R
SIMINS LH
SIMMONS J
SIMMONS T
SIMONS HH
SIMONS WA
SIMPSON G
SIMPSON JA
SIMPSON JN
SIMPSON JO
SIMS HV
SINCLAIR D
SINCLAIR DW
SINCLAIR FJ
SKENE TH
SKINNER LJ
SKINNER R
SLATTERY DJ
SLATTERY PM
SLAVIN CFG
SLINGO G
SLOAN CJ
SMALE JJ
SMALLHORN WL
SMART AJ
SMITH AE
SMITH AG
SMITH AG
SMITH AH
SMITH AP
SMITH B
SMITH GH
SMITH GP
SMITH GW
SMITH H
SMITH HP
SMITH J
SMITH JA
SMITH K
SMITH OW
SMITH PK
SMITH RG
SMITH SE
SMITH SR
SMITH TP
SMITH W
SMITH W
SMITH W
SMITH WJ

SMITH WK
SOMMERVILLE JP
SPAIN RGS
SPANG PH
SPARKES J
SPARKS GT
SPEARING W
SPEERS HLA
SPELLMAN H
SPINKS WE
SPORTE HM
SPOTTISWOOD JA
SPREADBOROUGH G
SPREADBURY GCF
SPREIZEN A
STACK DAFG
STALEY AG
STANBOROUGH
WH
STANDEN WC
STANDISH B
STANDRING A
STANLEY E
(also known as Stanley
Edward Kennedy)
STANLEY EJ
STANLEY J
STANLEY S
STANLEY-LOW HW
STAPLES AW
STAPLES FJ
STATT GWB
STEELE LW
STEER J
STEPHENS RW
STEPHENS TS
STEPHENS WI
STEPHENSON C
STETTLER JH
STEVENS CG
STEVENS G
STEVENS TC
STEWART CL
STEWART HA
STEWART JC
STEWART TS
STILWELL SW
STITT DH
STOCK GH
STOKES AE
STOKES W
STOREN LA
STORER F
STORNHEIM A

STRAFFORD JT
STRAHAN R
STRAKER GE
STRANGE HK
STRATTON R
STREFFORD E
STYLES EG
STYLES WHG
SULLIVAN AC
SULLIVAN J
SUMMERS J
SUMMERS JW
SUMMONS J
SUMNERS D
SUNDERLAND A
SUNDERMAN LA
SUNDSTRUM G
SUTCLIFFE ES
SUTHERLAND AC
SUTHERLAND RA
SUTHERLAND WB
SUTTERBY HR
SWAIN T
SWAINE W
SWANSON GT
SWANSTON EA
SWINBURNE TP
SWORDS JW
TABB OF
TAIT WJ
TANNER WJ
TASSELL LH
TATT TC
TAYLOR CB
TAYLOR CG
TAYLOR CRJ
TAYLOR CS
TAYLOR CT
TAYLOR EG
TAYLOR G
TAYLOR GA
TAYLOR GW
TAYLOR HH
TAYLOR HW
TAYLOR LD
TAYLOR RO
TAYLOR WR
TEASDALE W
TEASDALE WJ
TEEFER LJ
TENNANT WA
THATCHER CW
THEW E
THOMAS A

THOMAS AC
THOMAS C
THOMAS CH
THOMAS J
THOMAS JEB
THOMAS JH
THOMLINSON W
THOMPSON ER
THOMPSON H
THOMPSON HG
THOMPSON J
THOMPSON J
THOMPSON JL
THOMPSON L
THOMPSON RH
THOMSON FMcL
THOMSON JJ
THOMSON JC
THORBURN JM
THORPE TA
THYNE H
TIEMAN SG
TINK PCP
TIPPET CG
TODD GW
TOLL GW
TONER WPB
TONNESON W
TOPHAM JE
TRAINOR CE
TRAINOR WP
TRANGMAR HT
TRAVERS EH
TREACY JL
TREAHY JW
TREGENZA G
TREMBLETT JE
TRENWITH E
TROTMAN H
TROTT GG
TROTT W
TRUEMAN SH
TRUSLER RH
TUITE B
TURNBULL JC
TURNER AC
TURNER BB
TURNER EH
TURNER H
TURNER TE
TURNER WL
TURNO P
TWINING CF
TWITT VG

TWOMEY FO'C
UNDERWOOD JP
UPTON R
URRY GA
VASSIE GI
VAUGHAN FW
VEAL ET
VENVILLE WG
VERNON A
VERNON J
VICKERS TW
VIGAR G
VILLIERS AE
VIRGO TD
VOSS WL
WADDINGTON HL
WADSWORTH AB
WAEKE W
WAITE EW
WAKE JE
WALDRON LB
WALKER A
WALKER AG
WALKER HA
WALKER LA
WALKER LS
WALKER LS
WALKER PH
WALKER RO
WALKER S
WALKER VL
WALKINGTON WC
WALL JRB
WALLACE A
WALLACE DN
WALLACE J
WALLER J
WALLIS A
WALLIS CG
WALLIS E
WALLS JM
WALLS M
WALSH WM
WARD HD
WARD JD
WARD S
WARDLE E
WARDLE RW
WARNE W
WARRELL H
WARREN C
WARREN S
WASHBOURNE LE
WATERMAN WH

WATERS EJ
WATHEN SE
WATSON AG
WATSON BJ
WATSON E
WATSON TH
WATT IC
WATTS FG
WATTS H
WATTS HJ
WATTS J
WATTS LE
WATTS W
WAUGH RG
WAYCOTT GP
WEATE OC
WEBB JM
WEBB JM
WEBB PG
WEBB R
WEBLEY TK
WEBSTER AN
WEBSTER HA
WEBSTER J
WEIDNER VJM
WEIR CS
WELCH AE
WELCH WE
WELLS AH
WELLS FST
WELLS G
WELSH AD
WELSH LT
WELSHMAN MMG
WERRY ET
WESTAWAY HL
WESTERN AL
WESTHEAD T
WESTHEAD W
WESTWOOD AG
WHADCOAT DD
WHEATON SN
WHEELER DE
WHILEY CJH
WHIMPEY AE
WHIMPEY AR
WHITE DH
WHITE EWB
WHITE H
WHITE HH
WHITE JG
WHITE JS
WHITE JW
WHITE NB

WHITE RW
WHITE WA
WHITEWAY SH
WHITELAW AB
WHITELAW AV
WHITELEY AC
WHITELEY LC
WHITELEY TA
WHITEMAN HE
WHITEN C
WHITFIELD FJ
WHITFIELD WH
WHITMARSH WH
WHITTINGHAM EW
WICKS JH
WIGHTMAN S
WIGHTWOOD EG
WIGLEY GC
WILCOCK CEL
WILCOCK J
WILCOCK WVH
WILD C
WILKINSON AJ
WILKINSON EE
WILKINSON J
WILKINSON RN
WILKINSON TE
WILLIAMS A
WILLIAMS AE
WILLIAMS AJ
WILLLIAMS AJ
WILLIAMS AM

WILLIAMS BE
WILLIAMS CE
WILLIAMS CW
WILLIAMS E
WILLIAMS EG
WILLIAMS ER
WILLIAMS ET
WILLLIAMS F
WILLLIAMS GM
WILLLIAMS HS
WILLIAMS IH
WILLIAMS J
WILLIAMS JF
WILLIAMS JJ
WILLIAMS R
WILLIAMS RJ
WILLIAMS SW
WILLLIAMS WJ
WILLIS B
(also known as
A E Smith)
WILLIS H
WILLIS J
WILLMETT NR
WILLMOTT DH
WILLMOTT SW
WILLOUGHBY RT
WILLY G
WILMOT AJ
WILMOT HC
WILMOT LJ
WILSON EW

WILSON FP
WILSON GL
WILSON GS
WILSON HG
WILSON J
WILSON J
WILSON J
WILSON JG
WILSON LJ
WILSON NG
WILSON RA
WILSON SG
WILSON T
WINDRUS LA
(also known as
L A Garrett)
WINES SB
WINNELL GF
WINROW A
WINSOR FA
WINTLE WH
WISHART D
WITHERS AAA
WITHERS T
WITTINGSLOW CW
WITTINGSLOW TG
WOLSTENHOLME RF
WOOD A
WOOD S
WOODFIELD A
WOODHOUSE JR
WOODLAND A

WOODMAN R
WOODS H
WOODS HMcM
WOODS JP
WOODS
WOODYARD EV
WOOLCART FC
WOOLLEY HE
WOOTON HH
WOOTON NE
WOOTTON SE
WORSLEY F
WRAY HMcD
WRIGHT C
WRIGHT J
WRIGHT NSMcL
WRIGHT TJ
WYLIE KLG
WYND A
WYNDHAM IE
WYNNE T
YANDELL AC
YANDELL H
YAPP RTE
YARDLEY J
YARE W
YATES H
YATES JO
YOUNG AL
YOUNG JL
YOUNG WH
ZIEMAN EJ